THE *Spirituality* OF WINE

TOM HARPUR

THE *Spirituality* OF WINE

Northstone

Concept: Northstone Team
Editor: Michael Schwartzentruber
Industry consultant: Howard Soon, Calona Vineyards Wine Master
Cover and interior design: Margaret Kyle
Proofreading: Dianne Greenslade
Photo credits: see page 159

NORTHSTONE PUBLISHING is an imprint of WOOD LAKE
BOOKS INC. Wood Lake Books acknowledges the financial support
of the Government of Canada, through the Book Publishing Industry
Development Program (BPIDP) for its publishing activities.

WOOD LAKE BOOKS is an employee-owned company, committed
to caring for the environment and all creation. Wood Lake Books
recycles, reuses, and encourages readers to do the same. Resources
are printed on recycled paper and more environmentally friendly
groundwood papers (newsprint), whenever possible. The trees used
are replaced through donations to the Scoutrees For Canada Program.
A percentage of all profit is donated to charitable organizations.

National Library of Canada Cataloguing in Publication
Harpur, Tom
The spirituality of wine / Tom Harpur.
Includes bibliographical references.
ISBN 1-896836-63-1
1. Wine – Religious aspects. 2. Wine and wine making – History.
3. Spiritual life. I. Title.
BL457.W5H37 2004   204   C2004-902469-8

Published by Northstone Publishing
an imprint of WOOD LAKE BOOKS, INC.
9025 Jim Bailey Road, Kelowna, BC, Canada, V4V 1R2
250.766.2778
www.northstone.com

Printing 10 9 8 7 6 5 4 3 2 1
Printed in Canada by Friesens

The Spirituality of Wine

The Spirituality of Wine

Contents

Wine is God's special drink.
The purpose of good wine is to inspire us
to a livelier sense of gratitude to God.

JOHN CALVIN, 1509–1564

PROTESTANT REFORMER

The Spirituality of Wine

ACKNOWLEDGMENTS

This book has been a great joy to all who have participated in shaping and bringing it to full maturity. To everyone, from the Northstone team who originated the concept, to those responsible for the final design and editing, in particular the senior editor, Mike Schwartzentruber, and art director, Margaret Kyle, his gifted wife, the warmest of thanks. It was great fun to be back in harness as a team again. Many others also deserve to be acknowledged, but two persons specially stand out. Howard Soon is a winemaker true. But he also has a wisdom and an eye for detail that greatly assisted in keeping the text technically accurate. I extend my appreciation for his always prompt assistance. Finally, with her unfailing support and her untiring devotion to producing the most professional of final draft versions, there was my wife and associate in all my projects, Susan. A hearty toast to all of you!

– TOM HARPUR

Prologue

Sharing is second nature to wine lovers.
Show interest and a winemaker
will lead you into the cellar
and introduce you to all "his children."

TONY ASPLER – *VINTAGE CANADA*

My first serious introduction to wine came about as a result of one of those "happenstances" of life that turn out to have a deeper meaning. Carl Jung called these occurrences synchronicities, the more than merely frivolous or accidental coming together of significant events.

I was sitting alone in a matchless antique dining room in a large, historic hotel, the Hotel Splendide, in the center of the famous French wine city of Bordeaux. The year was 1972. It was early April, just before the grapes began to bud. The workers in the vineyards had been busy pruning the vines all day and the nostalgic, ageless scent of burning clippings had been drifting gently in the wind outside the doors as I had entered the hall.

I was there at the request of the publisher of *The Toronto Star*, who wanted me to "travel the world a while" to research and write a series on the issue of "quality of life" for modern men and women. I had come to Bordeaux to interview the great French philosopher and writer Jacques Ellul. Ellul had once fought in the French Resistance Movement and had later served as Mayor of Bordeaux. His studies on the impact of technology on human thought and behavior had made him internationally famous.

As I began to eat in this solitary splendor, a second guest was shown in by the head waiter and seated at the table next to mine. The moment he began to speak to the waiter I realized from his accent that he, too, was a Canadian.

I waited a reasonable time before intruding on his dinner by introducing myself. By a curious chance, it turned out that he was the officer in charge of catering all food and wine for Canada's then vibrantly successful Wardair airline and that he was in Bordeaux to meet with members of the famous Cruse wine-making family. His purpose was to facilitate the first-ever passenger-jet load of Bordeaux wines to be flown to Canada for use on the company's international flights. There was an empty Wardair plane waiting in Paris and the plan was to bring it to Bordeaux and to fill every empty seat and space on it not with passengers and baggage, but with cases of top quality claret.

When he heard I was a journalist, he eagerly invited me to cover the unique event for *The Star*. I explained to him the nature of my special beat – not general reporting, but religion and ethics. To my surprise he said, "Look, the publicity doesn't matter. In fact, I'm having dinner with the Cruse family tomorrow night. Would you like to come along as a guest?"

I leaped at the chance and will never forget the experience not just of meeting with my gracious hosts, but of dining in one of the most quietly magnificent dining rooms of any home I have ever been in. It was a centuries-old, chateau-like building and the room in which we met and had dinner was reminiscent of the hall of a medieval castle – but cozier. There were mounted heads of game animals on the walls and the ancient silver gleamed in the warm glow of scores of candles.

Different wines were served in modest amounts five or six times throughout the exquisite meal, each specially chosen for a particular course, with a tiny taste of sorbet in between to cleanse the palate in preparation for the next selection. All the wine I had ever tasted previously faded into nothingness. Matched by the witty, wide-ranging conversation and by the delicious, gourmet cuisine, it made for the kind of evening one might find described in a romantic novel.

When our host, Lionel Cruse, learned that I had never before visited a wine estate, he insisted that it was time I did. The next day, to my delight and pleasure, a driver and car appeared at the hotel at 9:30 a.m. and we spent the entire morning and afternoon visiting several of the Cruse chateaus and estates; visiting cavernous wine cellars; tasting

Of all drinks, wine is most profitable, of medicines most pleasant, and of dainty viands most harmless…
PLUTARCH, *MORALS*
(C. 46 – C. 120 CE)

11

The Spirituality of Wine

various exquisite vintages of the rich, red wine; and observing every aspect of the wine-making art that was operating at that season of the year. We visited two chateaus in the world-famous wine-growing area of the Gironde, the large estuary formed by the junction of the Garonne and Dordogne rivers, north of Bordeaux, and then stopped for lunch at an outdoor café at St. Emilion. The day was sunny and warm and we had a sweeping view southward across the Dordogne and the vine-filled valley lands of Entre-deux-Mers. My guide pointed out that this latter region lies, with four other equally storied wine districts, between the two great river valleys. South of that again, a luxurious countryside gently slopes southward to Sauternes.

This experience did not make me a wine expert by any stretch of the imagination. But it gave me a unique experience of one of the oldest of all human activities and a foretaste quite literally of heaven itself! The tastes, the smells, the venerable overseers and workers, the curving sweep of the vast vineyards beside the sea and the sense that something quite magical was in the air – none of this has ever left me. It all floats vividly through my mind today as I begin to write about the spirituality of wine.

Give me a bowl of wine: I have not that alacrity of spirit, Nor cheer of mind, that I was wont to have.

SHAKESPEARE, *RICHARD III*

13

1

The First Sip

A meal without wine is like a day without sunshine.
ANTHELME BRILLAT-SAVARIN, 1755–1826
FRENCH AUTHOR, GOURMET, & LAWYER

Wine is heavenly, both literally and as metaphor. Like Shakespeare's "quality of mercy," it "droppeth as the gentle rain from heaven upon the place beneath." It comes first from the sky as warm drops of rain; it flows from heavenly realms as a miracle and gift of God. Simultaneously, it is a blessing of nature's bounty and a reward for human ingenuity and toil. Nothing embodies and connects the synergy of human endeavor with the energies of the natural world of creation as this most ancient product of the earth. No other agricultural pursuit from the dawn of time has more truly portrayed, and at the same time sacramentally conveyed, the essence of the deepest spiritual realities of our lives.

Nature at this point becomes more than Ralph Waldo Emerson's "symbol of spirit"; wine is both the manifestation and the bearer of spirit to the soul. That's why sacred literature, particularly the Bible, overflows with references to wine and wine-making. The vine is the tree most often cited in its pages – some 205 times. It's also why, from even earlier times, ancient Egyptian tombs and other monuments were covered with vivid depictions of every aspect of the wine-making process, from planting vines, to harvesting and crushing the grapes, to the presenting and drinking of the wine itself. Tombs of the Pharaohs were well-stocked with wine and *The Egyptian Book of the Dead* and other records show a deep belief that drinking wine was a vital, joyous part of any afterlife.

The purpose of drinking wine is not intoxication… The point of drinking wine is to get in touch with one of the major influences of Western civilization, to taste sunlight trapped in a bottle, and to remember some stony slope in Tuscany or a village by the Gironde.

JOHN MORTIMER,
*RUMPOLE AND
THE BLIND TASTING*

The Spirituality of Wine

The vine is the quintessential sacred plant or tree of all the old religions of the Near and Middle East. The chief gods of the Greco-Roman world, as both classical art and literature abundantly reveal, were the gods of wine known as Dionysus or Bacchus. Jesus, the gospels say, was called a "wine-bibber and a glutton" by his enemies, because he enjoyed the celebration of friendly company, good food, and good wine. According to John's gospel, at his first miracle in Cana by the Sea of Galilee, Jesus turned gallons of water into the finest wine the wedding guests had ever tasted. Like Bacchus before, Christ came to intoxicate humanity with the divine wine of "life abundant."

As the distinguished American statesman, scientist, and author, Benjamin Franklin, once said,

We hear of…water into wine…as a miracle.
But this conversion is, through the goodness of God,
made every day before our eyes. Behold the rain which
descends from heaven upon our vineyards,
and which incorporates itself with the grapes,
to be changed into wine; a constant proof
that God loves us and wants us to be happy.

The Spirituality of Wine

Intrinsic to the quality of the inner or spiritual life we possess – whether it be faith-based or not – is the role of heart and mind in making decisions. Every moment, every "now," is a time for decisions, great and small, unless we are asleep. There is a close parallel in the subtle, yet highly skilled art of making wine – especially fine wine, the very best. What the French call *terroir*, the right place, with the right soil, the proper amount of sun and rain, the best exposure to, yet at times protection from, the wind – choosing that place is the most important decision of all.

*Wine in itself
is an excellent
thing.*
Pope Pius XII

As the experts describe it, wine is a unique agricultural product in that its price often depends almost entirely on its place of origin – even down to one tiny, perhaps even ugly, dried-up little hill! The precise spot on earth chosen for the vineyard will ultimately be the key factor. Consider, though, the other decisions that must be made, such as the kind of vines to plant, or the time of day or even the exact hour to begin picking the grapes. As grapes ripen, the delicate balance of sugar, water, acids (tartaric and malic), and other trace elements change daily. As with our own lives, it's an ongoing, living process. The most appropriate mode of extracting the juice must be determined, whether crushing, pressing, or leaving the grapes to drip. The specific kinds of yeasts to use has to be decided (the natural yeasts already on the grapes are killed off by use of sulphur dioxide).

The magical aspect, the fermentation process, calls for decision-making at its sharpest – stopped too soon and the wine may be too sweet. Stopped too late and it could all end up as vinegar! What is needed through it all is an acute awareness of balance and of being in tune with the basic elements and rhythms of creation. No wonder the final product, truly appreciated and responsibly handled, promotes, and is a companion to, a rich and balanced quality of life.

Wine is a living
liquid containing
no preservatives.
Its life cycle
comprises youth,
maturity, old age,
and death.
When not treated
with reasonable
respect it will
sicken and die.

JULIA CHILD

21

They are not long, the days of wine and roses;
Out of a misty dream
Our path emerges for a while, then closes
Within a dream.
ERNEST DOWSON, 1867–1900

The Spirituality of Wine

WINE AND OUR LIFE CYCLE

Spirituality has been defined in many different ways by many different people. But most agree that it is profoundly about our human quest for a higher quality of life than mere existence. Spirituality is about one's inner life, about the ongoing search for depths of meaning and significance far beyond the grasp of our animal senses and instincts. It flows from a deep conviction that there are forces at work in the universe that call us to transcend our material limitations and to soar to higher realities on wings of imagination and inspiration. For some people, this quest will be religious; for others not. But one commonality abides. Like the enjoyment of wine, this journey of the spirit is an unending quest and an adventure. The delight is most often found in the search itself.

From earliest times, our ancestors saw a strong parallel between the repetitive life cycle of the vine and wine, and the seasons of human life itself. Wine, for example, has a harsh and some might say "untidy" start to its career: when the grapes are at their plumpest and fullest glory, their juice is crushed out of its protected womb and its "blood" is spilled. Wine is untried, fresh, untamed in its youth; gradually and patiently growing into the greater mellowness of middle age; and often becoming something truly unique and memorable in its "wisdom,"

Wine in moderation – not in excess, for that makes men ugly – has a thousand pleasant influences. It brightens the eye, improves the voice, imparts a new vivacity to one's thoughts and conversation.

CHARLES DICKENS
BARNABY RUDGE

before it finally declines and dies. With the vine, similar analogies were found. Its arrival on the scene is like that of our own eager childhood and early years. Then there are all the joys and vicissitudes of heat and cold, wind and rain, drought and storms, like those of our adolescence and our struggles to find and establish our way in life. Rupert Brooke (1887–1915) called it "the red, sweet wine of youth." Next, the mature vine bears fruit, becoming truly productive for itself and giving of its energies to others. Then comes death and dissolution – followed by a rising to a renewed life and a different "body."

But the imagery of wine and the vine is so rich and so far-reaching in its implications for human life that we have a quiver full of other

The Spirituality of Wine

"arrows" of light to aim, other layers of symbolism to explore. The seasons themselves through which the vine must pass in the annual round are parables rich in spiritual lore. Some are so obvious as to scarcely need comment: the budding forth of new life in the spring, with its message of resurrection, renewal, a fresh start, new discoveries on the spiritual path – all of it relevant and a potent reminder of what may be going on within our inner lives. Then summer, with its messages of shadow and sunshine; of quiet, patient endurance through the storms or parching heat – reminiscent of our own daily enjoyments and battles in the "heat and burden" of daily life. The poet Emily Dickinson (1830–1886) used the metaphor of the Eucharist to express her participation in the joy of summer: "Oh sacrament of summer days, Oh last communion in the haze…and thine immortal wine!"

Autumn, with its thickly clustered grapes and the first signs of the harvest, speaks to our souls of bearing "fruit" in our own lives – in small acts of compassion and kindness, perhaps in just being there for others, perhaps in various successes and accomplishments. But traditionally in sacred literature, it is a time both for thanksgiving and for self-assessment, or – to use a theological term – for judgment. Not by some stern sky-God above, but in the light of the spirit that God has placed within.

Finally, comes winter. The vine's leaves wither and fail, its life gone dormant all through the frosts, the snow, the ice, and the winter gales. It is a time of rest, of quiet reflection, of pausing before leaping forth to begin the cycle once again.

Winter, perhaps the one single factor that makes many Canadian wines unique and increasingly sought-after overseas, is a metaphor for those times in our spiritual lives when the spirit asks us simply to "sit still awhile," to "wait upon God" and learn something about endurance, patience, and ultimately hope. A vineyard in winter may seem bleak and sad and dreary to some. But for those with the eyes to see, it has a mysterious, secret beauty all its own. Just as often happens in our spiritual lives – when it seems that nothing is going on or that we're frozen inside, but the spirit is working deep within – so, too, with the vines. To our eyes, they seem to sleep. And they *do* sleep – but as they sleep they dream of springs and summers and autumn vintages yet to come. It is one of the most ancient, hallowed dreams of Earth. Vines, vineyards, and the wines they produce, all speak of the art of aging or maturing gracefully. This, like any truly spiritual process, can only happen when we have done our best and can then relax and trust those powers that lie beyond our culture's lust for close control. They cannot be forced or rushed. Good wine always speaks to us of that reality.

The Spirituality of Wine

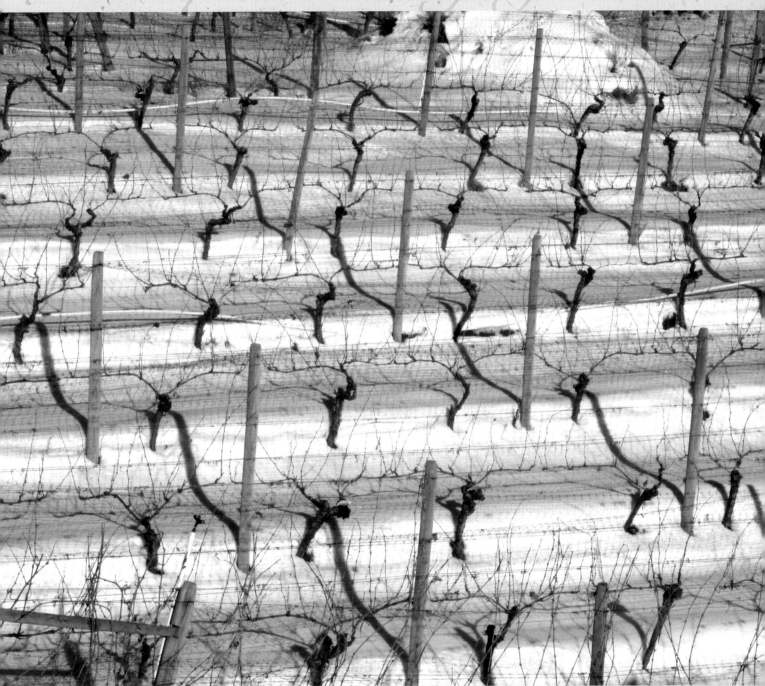

A vineyard in winter may seem bleak and sad and dreary to some… But for those with the eyes to see, it has a mysterious, secret beauty all its own. To our eyes, they seem to sleep. And they do sleep — but as they sleep they dream of springs and summers and autumn vintages yet to come. It is one of the most ancient, hallowed dreams of Earth.

2

The Universal Connection

Wine is truly the nectar of the gods…
like the Incarnation it is both human and divine.
Wine is divine, a gift of God.

PAUL TILLICH,
GERMAN-AMERICAN THEOLOGIAN, UNION THEOLOGICAL SEMINARY, NEW YORK

Nobody knows how or by whom wine was first discovered. But in its most basic form it is the near-miraculous, spontaneous result of fermentation – the interaction between yeast and the sugar in the juice of a crushed grape that produces alcohol and carbon dioxide. All it really takes is for the grape's skin to break. Since 20–30 percent of the grape's pulp is sugar and since there are natural yeasts both in the air around us and on the skin of the

The Spirituality of Wine

Wine, the most
delightful of
drinks, whether
we owe it
to Noah, who
planted the vine,
or to Bacchus,
who pressed juice
from the grape,
goes back
to the childhood
of the world.

ANTHELME BRILLAT-SAVARIN
LA PHYSIOLOGIE DU GOUT

grape itself, we can imagine the day when one of our remote ancestors discovered that some bruised grapes that had been put in a bark or stone or animal skin container had remarkably changed overnight. Tasting and drinking some of the juice, this ancestor awakened to a pleasant, not to say ecstatic experience, and what is perhaps the most fascinating story of all human experiments and developments began to unfold.

We will be looking at the sweeping history of wine-making shortly. But from the beginning, the wine process seemed like a form of magic, a gift of the gods. Its effects were like those of a mystical, divine breath. Our early ancestors quickly learned how to safeguard and improve the fundamental process. Today's detailed technical control of the rate of fermentation, temperatures, methods of storing, and so much more, are highly sophisticated indeed. But ultimately these are minor tunings of what is primarily a profoundly natural phenomenon guided with infinite care.

WINE AND WORSHIP

Significantly, wine very quickly replaced water as the basic liquid used in early worship and was utilized both as sacred drink and as an offering. The color of red wine spoke deeply of our own life's blood. The crushing of grapes thus vividly symbolized sacrifice. The pouring out of libations (wine offerings) symbolized the outpouring of divine energies, of divine life being distributed to mortals. The mild headiness and elevation of spirits it brought denoted heavenly ecstasy – Plato's divine "mania" itself.

Wine's efficacy in changing and elevating consciousness was thus attributed to supernatural spirits or gods. This led naturally to

The Spirituality of Wine

the incorporation of wine into the major rites of various religions – particularly those of the ancient Middle East and the Mediterranean basin.

For example, Judaism incorporated the drinking of wine from its earliest times and at every stage of its development. Wine was used to sanctify the altar and was itself an offering to God and a means of celebrating the divine presence and bounty. Today, wine plays a key part in all ceremonies and rites of passage, from the circumcision of a baby boy at eight days, to the toasting of the soul of the departed at death. In between, wine is ever-present: at weddings, at the beginning and ending of every Sabbath and festival, and particularly, at Passover with its four rounds of the cup – and always there is the extra, special cup for the prophet Elijah, symbolic of the hope of the coming of the Messiah.

WINE AND THE PRESENCE OF THE DIVINE

The first mention of wine in the Bible comes almost immediately after the story of the great deluge in Genesis, where the text tells us that Noah "began to be a husbandman and he planted a vineyard." Behind this great mythical epic there is a deeply esoteric or hidden inner symbolism and meaning. The name Noah comes from the same root word as the Greek word for mind – *nous*. Our English words noetic and noumenal come from this as well. Thus, the inner meaning understood by the ancient sages was that the divine mind was beginning the world anew after the flood and for this reason gave the gift of the vine and of wine-making to humanity. It signified divine inspiration for our species in the new cycle about to begin.

Another insight into the connection between spirit and wine is contained in a strange passage found early in the Genesis account of Abraham, the symbolic father of three great world religions: Judaism, Christianity, and Islam. In this passage, there is a battle, which the patriarch wins. Immediately afterwards he is met by a mysterious priest-king of Salem, who "brought forth bread and wine" and gave him a blessing. This is the first biblical hint and reference to the close relationship between bread and wine, and to the many-layered spiritual significance of their near-universal use in divine and human bonding.

The Spirituality of Wine

But the origin of these ideas is much older than even the Bible itself. Behind all the pagan wine celebrations, even when taken to excess, was the message of the legitimate and blessed ecstasy of the human soul partaking of the heavenly or spiritual wine from above. The presence of wine and its potency was at the deepest level a symbol of the presence of the incarnated god or the divine soul within us all.

In the wall-paintings adorning Egyptian tombs and in Egyptian friezes, images of wine-making – from planting, to harvesting, to treading the ripe grapes to crush out the juice – stand as a constant metaphor and reminder of the ongoing spiritual processes in humans. Horus (son of Osiris and Isis) was the Egyptian god of wine, and, at an annual festival, intoxication was celebrated as a symbol of the effect of imbibing the spiritual "liquor" of divine life within. In the Egyptian "Eucharist," the juice or "blood" of the grape represented Horus' essential energy. Horus also speaks of himself as the "true vine" of which his followers are the branches, just as Jesus does most powerfully in chapter 15 of the gospel of John, centuries later:

I am the true vine, and my Father is the vinegrower…
I am the vine, you are the branches…

JOHN 15:1, 5

*Eat this bread,
drink this cup…*

In other words, in the Christian faith, the vine is the leading metaphor for the relationship between the Christ and his followers, just as wine was and remains the essential metaphor for his "blood" or life energy in each.

In fact, the point of the well-known story in John's gospel about Jesus turning water into wine was to show that a greater god of wine had arrived than either Dionysus or Bacchus, the Greco-Roman gods of wine.

It should also be clear from the above that the central Christian sacrament of Holy Communion involving bread and wine, symbolizing and sacramentally *giving* the energies of Christ's blood or life force, did not originate with the early church, but with these much more ancient traditions.

The great classical scholar Thomas Taylor says that the pressing of grapes is "an evident symbol" of the dispersion of divine energy into *all* humanity. Since many drink from this one source, it symbolizes – like Paul says of the one "loaf" at Holy Communion – humanity's fundamental, underlying unity and potential harmony.

The cup [of wine] of blessing which we bless, is it not the communion of the blood [essential energies] of Christ? The bread which we break, is it not the communion of the body of Christ? For we being many are one bread, and one body…

1 CORINTHIANS 10:16 (KJV)

The Spirituality of Wine

*Wine is one of
the noblest
cordials
in nature.*
JOHN WESLEY

WINE IN THE STARS

Long before the Egyptians had ever committed anything to writing,
they had created in their oral mythology elaborate uranospheres or
planispheres depicting the whole of life in the starry heavens above.
The constellation Orion striding across the heavens stood for the ever-
coming *Christos* or Christ and the cluster of grapes in the heavens (in
or near the sign Virgo) and the stars configuring Orion's Crater or
Goblet emphasized the centrality of wine imagery for their faith. Many
centuries later, Christian missionaries and explorers traveling in remote
parts of the world were often amazed to find similar religious uses of
bread and wine by native priests and shamans.

WINE AND SOCIAL EASE

In antiquity, wine facilitated social communication and harmony much as it does today. We know from pottery shards, tablets, inscriptions, and the arts, for instance, that wine very quickly became central to the most cherished personal and social ceremonies of ancient peoples, and especially to their rites of passage, as mentioned above. Wine was ubiquitous at births, initiations of all kinds, marriages, the negotiation of compacts or business contracts, feasts, conclaves, coronations of royalty, magical rituals, worship, and funerals.

Socially, wine helped to allay fears, to reduce anxieties, hostilities, and tensions. And so at times it acted as a balm to cool social unease. Occasionally, in a formalized way, it was used to vent potentially disruptive hostilities in the community. In other words, it had the power to bring about mood changes in various desired directions.

The use of wine to ease social interaction remains prevalent today, and is no less powerful than it was in ages past. Offering wine to visitors, to the "stranger," or to one's host, is a symbolic announcement of intended friendship, peace, and agreement. In this way, it remains a "socio-activating medicine."

RELIGIOUS ECSTASY AND MYSTICISM

*[Wine] brings individuals together outside their
accustomed social and economic roles, to savor something
of exquisite beauty that has no utilitarian purpose other
than the grace it sheds upon our appreciation of life.*

ROBERT C. FULLER, *RELIGION AND WINE*

Ancient religious and secular texts alike contained warnings against the abuse of wine, but there were times when intoxication was encouraged as a special way of marking the way in which divine incarnation – the coming of divine spirit into the life of every mortal – lifted one out of oneself to other, higher contacts and perceptions. This was true in Egyptian life, at the yearly Uaaka or harvest festival in ancient times, and it was also true in the Greco-Roman era, in Bacchanalian revelries at specific times of the year. In general, then, it's fair to say that ancient religions tended to use wine to induce religious ecstasy and hence communion with the higher powers.

Today, major religious traditions – Roman Catholic, Anglican/ Episcopal, Lutheran, Eastern Orthodox, and Jewish – tend to restrict the role of wine to its more sacramental uses. And yet there is still a

The Spirituality of Wine

mystical aspect to the tasting and drinking of wine that raises the human spirit to new heights. William James, in his famous book *The Varieties of Religious Experience,* says that mild alcohol intoxication produces a distinct, altered state of consciousness that must be "considered one bit of the mystic consciousness" of humans. Alcohol, he tells us, has the power "to stimulate the mystical faculties of human nature that are usually crushed to earth by the cold facts and dry criticism of the sober hour... It is the great exciter of the *Yes* function in [humanity]... It makes [us] for the moment one with the truth."

What James describes here is the power of wine to bring our ego and the objects beyond it together. The result is a mystical sense of wonder. This is particularly true in the way in which wine enriches our appreciation of the whole of creation. As Robert Fuller, who provides the opening quote on the previous page, goes on to stress, there is a moral and spiritual dimension – a truly mystical experience – in the deep encounter with Nature.

*Give me
a bowl of wine —
in that I bury
all unkindness.*
WILLIAM SHAKESPEARE

43

TRANSFORMATION

Spirituality and wine, the life of the spirit and the miracle of the fermentation of the grape, are inextricably and even eternally connected. The gospel accounts of the Last Supper portray Jesus saying that he will not drink again of the fruit of the vine "until I drink it new with you in the [future] Kingdom of Heaven."

Dr. Alvin Boyd Kuhn, a renowned world religions scholar who died in 1963, wrote at length about the powerful significance of wine symbolism for ancient peoples. The spiritual theme in all of this, he suggests, is that the soul or "portion" of the divine within "causes a divine ferment in the body of life." It is perfected and matured there by the "sun" of our spiritual or true self and watered by the "rain" of God's blessing.

3

The Story of Wine

I within did flow
With seas of life,
like wine.

THOMAS TRAHERNE,
1637–1674

To take wine into your mouth
is to savor a droplet of the river of human history.

CLIFTON FADIMAN
THE NEW YORK TIMES, MARCH 8, 1987

EXOTIC ORIGINS

Wine was first discovered by a woman." With these seven pleasing words, wine historian William Younger begins his romantic account of the ages-old connection between wine, the Middle East, and Egypt. In his book *Gods, Men and Wine*, he tells a lovely story, retold in varying versions by wine experts, about a mythological Persian king named Jemsheed who had a passionate fondness for grapes. Jemsheed regularly had the grapes stored in stone bowls or jars, so as to have a ready supply at hand throughout the long

winter months. As they dried out, of course, the grapes became sweet
raisins. One day, however, he discovered that the grapes in a particular
jar were sweet no longer (they had fermented). Thinking that the liquid
in the jar was poisonous, he had it labeled as such.

The Spirituality of Wine

But a member of his harem who suffered from excruciating headaches had taken notice. One night, desperate with her unbearable pain and resolved to end her suffering by any means, she quaffed some of the "poison." Instantly, she became drowsy, fell asleep, and woke not long afterwards feeling a rare sense of well-being. She went back, drank the remainder of the liquid in the jar, and, completely refreshed, decided to describe her experience to Jemsheed.

Upon hearing her words, Jemsheed ordered his servants to make a large quantity of the new beverage and he drank it with all his courtiers. He was reputed to have gone on to live 700 years!

Younger admits the undoubtedly "poetic" nature of the story, but notes that in the Sumerian epic of Gilgamesh, one of the world's oldest poems, a close connection is indeed made between a woman and the first wine-making.

The same motif continues in antiquity. The Sumerian (very ancient Babylon) goddess of wine was Gestin and a clay tablet from Ugarit on the coast of Syria tells how a woman helped a hero-god first cultivate the vine there. In Egypt in the 15th century BCE, female deities presided over the wine-making.

> *Wine was given us of God, not that we might be drunken, but that we might be sober; that we might be glad, not that we get ourselves pain.*
>
> ST. JOHN CHRYSOSTOM
> *HOMILIES*

49

The Neolithic Age

In truth, wine-making is as old as the history of civilization itself. It first emerges out of the mists of antiquity, even before the Neolithic Period (8500–4000 BCE). Wine scholars say that the undomesticated wild grape, *genus vitis*, is truly a primeval plant, with the fossil records showing it in tertiary strata of the Earth from a million to 60 million years ago.

Fossils show that there were several species of wild vines groping and searching for support on rocks, shrubs, and bushes in Iceland, the Rhineland, and parts of France long before there was any animal life on the planet. Today, the descendants of those vines make up 16 North American varieties. But it is Europe's lone branch of the family, *vitis vinifera* (literally the wine-bearing vine), that remains the only one from which all of the world's better wines are made. In several thousand varieties (varietals), it flourishes now in the temperate zones of all civilized countries of the northern and southern hemispheres. But it was there at the very beginning waiting expectantly for our species to make its appearance.

Archaeologists now estimate that the earliest forms of wine were probably being made at least 10,000 years ago. Indeed, it can be said that when preliterate, prehistoric humans first came on the scene

The Spirituality of Wine

– dreaming, loving, working, worrying human beings very much like ourselves – they did so accompanied by some corn cakes or loaves of bread, and a rude jar of wine. A Neolithic "cuisine" began to flower and an essential part of it was wine.

In any case, the ancient Near East and Middle East, particularly the northern hills and valleys of ancient Persia (modern Iran) and northern Iraq, and then what later became known as Palestine, seem to have been the point of origin. Once nomadic lifestyles were replaced by more settled communities – in the fertile crescent of the Levant, in the upper Tigris-Euphrates Valley, and along the fertile delta of the Nile – a budding agriculture made possible a more leisurely pace of living. The arts blossomed. The Assyrian kings had elaborate wine cellars in their palaces. Religions that were closely tied to nature in terms of symbolism and inner meanings flourished everywhere and wine played a central role.

At a site recently excavated at Hajji Firuz Tepe, in the northern Zagros Mountains of Iran, several clay jars each with a volume of about 9 litres (2.5 gallons) were found embedded along the wall of what was once a kitchen in a Neolithic mud building. The jars contained residues which proved to be wine-based. The building dates from the period 5400–5000 BCE, but the appearance of pottery vessels around 6000 BCE had made possible the longer storage of wine at least 600 years earlier.

The Spirituality of Wine

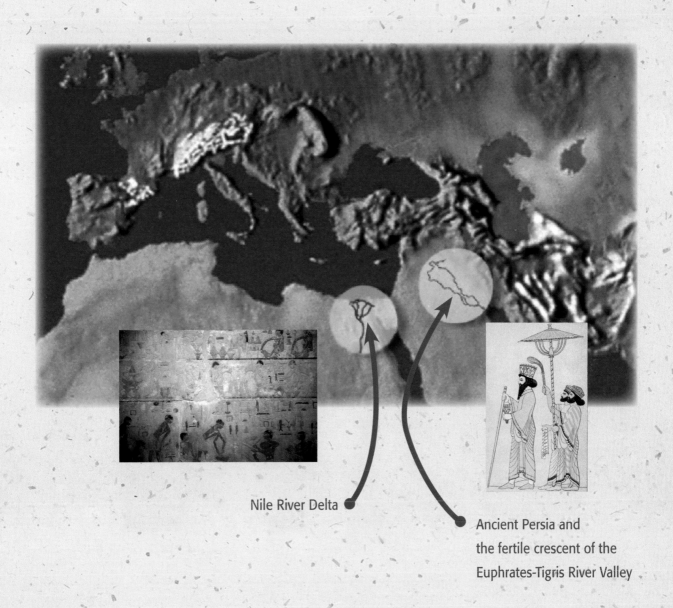

Nile River Delta

Ancient Persia and
the fertile crescent of the
Euphrates-Tigris River Valley

The Romance of Trade

...a cargo of ivory, and apes and peacocks,
sandalwood, cedarwood
and sweet white wine.
John Masefield, 1878–1967

Experts estimate that Early Bronze Age trade between Egypt and Palestine – comprising modern Israel, the West Bank and Gaza, and Jordan – led to the establishment of vineyards in the Nile Delta by at least the Third Dynasty (c. 2700 BCE). Some scholars put it much earlier, around 4000 BCE. The industry soon spread to the western oases and to towns in the Upper Nile.

Vast amounts of wine were buried in the tombs of the Pharaohs at Abydos and Saqqara, the chief religious centers, as a symbol of the wine expected in the afterlife. Seal impressions on clay lumps pressed over the wine-jar lids gave the name of the Pharaoh entombed – the very first wine labels! Apparently, they believed in the truth expressed by novelist George Meredith:

The Spirituality of Wine

A house with a great wine stored below
lives in our imagination as a joyful house,
fast and splendidly rooted in the soil.

Wine is a
magician,
for it loosens
the tongue and
liberates good
stories.
HOMER

Vines, the vintner's art, and wine itself played a prominent part in ancient Egyptian art, and particularly in Egyptian theology or spirituality, as we have already seen. Nothing reveals this spiritual connection more vividly than the 130-foot long Harris Papyrus, which lists the ancient temples of Egypt and shows that in the reign of Ramses III they owned a total of 513 vineyards. Archaeologists have found conical vases or jars in tombs each showing the date, origin, and mark of an inspector on them – a forerunner of our modern quality ratings systems. Tombs and other monuments are covered with scenes of every stage of wine-making. The symbolism was profoundly spiritual throughout. In fact, wine very quickly took on the aura of sacred drink in all the religions of the Mediterranean, and in all the Middle Eastern hinterland.

The evidence is everywhere in the literature, and in the depictions of songs and dances – wine was integral to the good and holy life.

One barrel of wine can work more miracles than a church full of saints.

OLD ITALIAN PROVERB

The Spirituality of Wine

THE GREEKS

The wine urges me on, the bewitching wine,
which sets even a wise man to singing and
to laughing gently and rouses him up to dance…

HOMER

THE ODYSSEY, XIV, 1.463

Many centuries later, the "Father of History," Herodotus, writing c. 485–425 BCE, describes the shipping of wine down the Tigris and the Euphrates Rivers from Armenia. Round skin boats were loaded with date-palm casks of wine for delivery to Babylon and other centers. Using ships and well-traveled overland routes, Phoenician and Greek traders carried vines, wine-making, and wine, all over the ancient world, as early as 1000 BCE. The Greeks who were great colonizers – going east, up into the Caspian and Baltic Oceans, and west to Italy and beyond the Pillars of Hercules (Gibraltar) – planted grapes and sold wine wherever they went. This is probably how cultivated grapes first came to Italy, Sicily, Andalusia, and North Africa, setting the stage for the eventual establishment of some of the most famous and productive vineyards the world has ever known.

Here are some insights into the Greek view of wine:

Wine, dear boy, and truth.
[This is the earliest known reference
to what became the proverb
in vino veritas — "In wine there is truth."]
ALCAEUS, 625–575 BCE
FRAGMENT 66

Wine is a peep-hole on a person.
ALCAEUS
FRAGMENT 104

It is better to hide ignorance, but it is hard to do this
when we relax over wine.
HERACLITUS, 540–480 BCE

For filled with that good gift [wine] suffering mankind
forgets its grief; from it comes sleep, with it oblivion of the
troubles of the day. There is no other medicine for misery.
EURIPIDES, 485–406 BCE

The Spirituality of Wine

THE ROMANS

*Wine is the drink
of the gods.*
JOHN STUART BLACKIE,
1809–1895
SCOTTISH SCHOLAR

The ancient Greek name for Italy meant "the land that produces wine"!

Millions of shattered amphorae (pottery jars), in which wine was once stored and shipped, are found today in ancient middens (refuse heaps) all over Italy. The Romans eventually invented round bottles and barrels as a more effective means of storage.

As the Roman Empire gradually replaced and outgrew that of the Greeks, vine cultivation expanded along with the Empire. In addition to their daily wine rations, marching soldiers of the Roman legions

59

routinely carried along young vines for planting. Thus these vines were introduced for the first time to Gaul, or France as we know it today. Often, however, all that was necessary was to teach the conquered peoples how to clear their riverbanks and hillsides of trees, and to prune and train the vines already growing.

Some of the finest vineyards in France – destined to be famous to the present day – were planted in Caesar's time, and were situated as far west as Bordeaux. In the Moselle Valley and in the Rhineland of Germany, the best vineyards date back to the years of early Roman occupation, as the Romans followed the natural flow of communications up the great river valleys of the Rhine, the Danube, the Rhone, and the Marne, to name a few. By the end of the second century CE, wine had come to Burgundy; in the third century, there were vines along the Loire; and by the fourth century, they were planted in Champagne; thus laying the basis for the greatest and most famous vineyards of the modern world.

Today there are literally thousands of books on wine, but even this tradition began far back in Roman times. The first known book on wine was written by Mago of Carthage (in Tunisia) near the end of the fourth century BCE. By the first century CE, Virgil, Horace, Cato, Varro, Columella, and Martila had all written books on wine, just to name a few.

The Spirituality of Wine

THE MIDDLE AGES

As the ancient world emerged out of the Dark Ages, the production and refinement of wine passed increasingly to the church. As early as the eighth century, Charlemagne, the Emperor of the West, gave full protection to the church and keenly encouraged viticulture by its clergy and monks. The churches identified even more fully with wine from the Middle Ages on, because for centuries it owned and cultivated the best vineyards of Europe.

As the monasteries grew in wealth, they expanded and took over what had once belonged to the former secular society. As places of continuous learning, they were repositories of the necessary skills and knowledge – and had the money, the labor, and the leisure – for continual technical development. Their desire to do "all to the glory of God" encouraged the evolution of ever greater and more uplifting standards of quality. Monastic orders developed the predecessors of modern grape varieties and experimented with the ancestors of today's best brandies and liqueurs.

Late in the 17th century, someone discovered the cork. It became clear that wine kept in a tightly corked bottle lasted longer than wine kept in a barrel; and it aged differently, acquiring a "bouquet."

61

Throughout this period, different wines had their day. Burgundy was favored in the 18th century, followed shortly afterwards by a wide variety of white wines. By the early 19th century, the demand was for long-fermented, dark-colored wine. By 1880, in Italy alone, 80 percent of the population more or less relied on some aspect of wine and its production for their living.

Then the terrible plague known as phylloxera struck. This tiny insect or mite, which is native to the United States and which attacks the roots of the vine, was inadvertently introduced to France in 1860. Soon, almost every vineyard in Europe became infested and the vines died. However, since certain native American vines had built up an immunity to this blight, European vine cuttings were grafted onto their roots and a new generation of vineyards was begun. Thus, the salvation and survival of *vitis vinifera* was wholly achieved by grafting it onto the roots of the North American, phylloxera-resistant *vitis labrusca*.

I wonder what the vintners buy one half so precious as the stuff they sell.
Omar Khayyam

The Spirituality of Wine

WESTWARD HO!

In 1562, French Huguenots sailed to Florida searching for the freedom to follow their Protestant religion. Almost at once they discovered that they were able to produce wine from native grapes they found there. In *Religion and Wine*, wine scholar Robert Fuller tells how similar Huguenot immigrants brought their wine-making skills to new colonies in Rhode Island, Virginia, Massachusetts, and Pennsylvania. The first English settlement in Jamestown in 1607 was growing grapes within two years. The Pilgrims who landed at Plymouth had probably already produced wine to celebrate their first thanksgiving in 1623.

There is no doubt, historians say, that the first Europeans coming to America – very religious people in the main – believed moderate use of alcohol to be an essential part of healthy living. For one thing, the drinking water was often suspect. By contrast, beverages such as cider, beer, and wine were much safer. And they not only warmed the body and aided digestion, but they raised a person's spirits in the face of the hazards of settlement in a harsh environment.

Contrary to what many might think, some of the early Puritans came to the New World well-laden with provisions of wine. For example, when the ship Arabella set out for Boston in 1630, filled with Puritans in search of religious freedom, it also carried 10,000 gallons of

Where there is no wine, love perishes, and everything else that is pleasant to [humanity].

EURIPIDES
THE BACCHAE

63

*The best kind
of wine is that
which is most
pleasant to him
who drinks it.*

PLINY THE ELDER
NATURAL HISTORY

wine and three times as much beer as water. Fuller tells us that by 1792 there were 2,579 distilleries in the United States, a figure which grew by the year 1810 to nearly 15,000. Taverns dispensing food and wine were an essential part of community life.

In truth, religion was a very powerful force in the spread of wine-making through the whole of the United States. Experts tell us that it played a vital role in early nation building and in the bonding of community life. Settlers coming from Germany and other Lutheran-influenced parts of Europe brought wine-making skills with them. For example, in the mid-1800s, the Amana colonies of Iowa had communal kitchens and regularly served wine at lunch and dinners. Local vintages were compared at regular Sunday after-church wine-tastings. The Amish of Pennsylvania founded vineyards that continue today. Wine and everything connected with it reinforced the bonds between people who saw each other at worship, at communal meals, and informal social gatherings.

Today, 90 percent of wine in the United States is grown in California, where Jesuits and Franciscans planted grapes in the early 18th century. People visiting California's vineyards today still follow a famous road that was once called The Mission Trail, El Camino Real, and The King's Highway. As the monks, led by Franciscan friar Father

The Spirituality of Wine

Junipero Serra, forged ever northward, they left 21 missions and vineyards in the most fertile areas. The trail began at San Diego and extended 500 miles up the coast to Sonoma. The Spanish grape they planted became known as the Mission grape.

Canada

The story of wine in Canada begins many centuries ago, in the early 11th century, when Leif Ericsson's Viking crew of 35 stalwart adventurers first sighted land and put ashore at his L'Anse aux Meadows in northern Newfoundland. They named the awesomely rugged island Vinland, or Winland, because of the abundance of vigorous wild grape vines in the gentler bays and coves. (Eventually the entire northeastern coast from Newfoundland to as far as south Virginia laid claim to this early title because of the proliferation of native grapes along the shores.)

In Canada, in the 17th and early 18th centuries, hardy explorers, followed by missionaries – mostly Jesuits – brought wine with them and, beginning in Nova Scotia, it was not long before tentative efforts to cultivate the native wild grapes were made. The first significant winery was established in the 1800s near the Credit River in what is now Mississauga, Ontario, by a Count Justin M. de Courtenay. In 1867, the year of Canada's Confederation, he won high commendation for his product at a major wine exposition in Paris. Shortly thereafter, by the 1890s, Pelee Island and the North Shore of Lake Erie had become the largest wine-producing region in the country. The Concord grape – developed near Concord, Ontario, and sometimes crossed with the Labrusca – became the mainstay for almost a century.

The Spirituality of Wine

The Spirituality of Wine

While much of Canada is not suited for wine production, the truly remarkable vineyards occur where there is a unique microclimate and the right soil. In British Columbia, for example, there are interior north-south valleys that run between the mountain ranges and that afford near-arid, continental conditions with cold winters and hot summers. The Okanagan Valley, with its long, deep lake is just such a prime site. Here again religion played a vital role.

Father Pandosy, an Oblate missionary, settled by Lake Okanagan in the early 1860s, close to what is now the thriving city of Kelowna. He planted a vineyard for sacramental wine and for his own table. It took until 1926, however, for the first commercial vineyard to be planted by J. W. Hughes, also near Kelowna. But the march towards world recognition and awards really began with the establishment in 1978 of British Columbia's first estate winery and the introduction of top grape varieties such as Riesling, Chardonnay, Pinot Blanc, Pinot Noir; and with the growth of the icewine phenomenon – wine made from frozen grapes in early winter. Canada's first icewine was made in 1978. Today, this product is the most sought-after Canadian wine by foreign buyers, especially those from Asia.

The Okanagan still holds more than 90 percent of the vine acreage in British Columbia, and most of the wineries. But from

a dozen wineries in 1983 the number now has grown to more than 50, with exciting new regions – the smaller Similkameen Valley, just west of the Okanagan; the Fraser River valley near Vancouver; and Vancouver Island and the nearby Gulf Islands – growing and improving constantly.

The Spirituality of Wine

Before the full arrival of the British Columbia and Nova Scotia wine regions, 85 percent of Canadian vineyards grew in Ontario. By the mid-1970s, a wide range of imported sophisticated European vine stocks and hybrid crossings changed the entire shape and character of the emerging wine industry. Today, Canadian Chardonnays, Merlots, Pinot Noirs, Pinot Grigios, Gamays, and especially icewines, routinely win top honors at international wine competitions. As wine critic Tony Aspler notes in *Vintage Canada*, "a style is evolving in Ontario and British Columbia that is unique to these growing regions and has nothing to do with California taste profiles, let alone those of France, Italy or Germany. Canadian white wines, both dry and sweet, have come of age…the reds are improving steadily and some…are very fine indeed." There are now well over 150 wineries across Canada in seven provinces (there are 80 in Ontario alone), and, as in the Okanagan Valley and elsewhere, they are still multiplying apace.

Incidentally, since with wine what counts most is *terroir* (the right place), it's significant that Pelee Island, Canada's largest estate-owned winery, with 600 acres of vineyards, is situated at Canada's southernmost point of inhabited land – the same latitude as many of the prime wine regions of the world, including the Napa Valley, in California; France; Italy; Germany; Portugal; and Spain.

AROUND THE WORLD

Speaking of Portugal and Spain, no survey of the spreading of wine culture would be complete without noting that the Portuguese introduced viticulture and the art of wine-making to Brazil, while the Spaniards brought both to Argentina, Chile, Peru, and Mexico in the 16th century. The Dutch did the same for South Africa in the 17th century, while the British exported the plants and the skills to Australia and New Zealand in the late 18th and early 19th centuries.

The Dutch experience in bringing wine-making to South Africa is a strikingly romantic tale. In Africa, viticulture is only possible at the extremes of the continent, though they did have palm wines, date wines, and other forms of fermented drinks from fruits. In April, 1652, Jan van Riebeeck and his ship the Drommedaris dropped anchor in a bay off the Cape of Good Hope and he rowed ashore to become the founder of the Dutch East India Company's first settlement at the southwestern tip of Africa. Three years later, the Dutch brought vines, along with various seed crops, and in 1669 Riebeeck was able to write in his journal, "Today, praise to God, wine was made for the first time from Cape grapes." The fabulous story of South African wines had begun.

The Spirituality of Wine

Today, wine is made in over 50 countries and is imported regularly in large amounts by about 50 others.

WINE AS CULTURE

The important thing to mark is that wine-growing and wine-drinking soon became part of a widespread agricultural and cultural pattern peculiar to the more temperate zones of the planet, where Mediterranean or "Western" humanity flourished. Wine production and enjoyment is deeply attached to the most widely spread, longest-lived civilization on Earth. And from its very beginning, it has been inextricably connected with our highest aspirations and the search for meaning itself. Wine and human spirituality represent two inseparable strands in the one thread of life. Not just the Sumerian, Egyptian, and Greco-Roman cultures, but Christian religious life as well was shot through with this connection between wine and the life of the innermost spirit.

Neither can there can be any question that the growth and flourishing of a culture surrounding wine over the past few decades both in the United States and in Canada has, as various observers have remarked, some distinct characteristics or traits of a genuinely spiritual movement. This represents a too-long neglected aesthetic side of North American life that Europe has known for generations.

If God forbade drinking, would he have made wine so good?
CARDINAL RICHELIEU

The Spirituality of Wine

PROHIBITION

*Prohibition more than anything else turned Canadians
into a nation of wine-drinkers.*

TONY ASPLER, *VINTAGE CANADA*

While throughout the ages wine has been central to most religions
– Islam is a noted exception – there have always been ascetic individuals
and groups who have focused more upon its dangers and upon isolated
scriptural warnings against the use of alcohol in general. Forgetting the
ancient wisdom that in all things "the potential for abuse never takes
away the legitimacy of proper use" (my translation of the Latin proverb,

The Spirituality of Wine

abusus non tollit usum), they have at times declared open warfare.

They have forgotten what Shakespeare says in *Othello:*

> *Come, come; good wine is*
> *a good familiar creature if it be well used.*

> *abusus non tollit usum*
> *The potential for abuse never takes away the legitimacy*
> *of proper use.*
> LATIN PROVERB

By the middle of the 19th century in the United States and Canada, the late 18th-century temperance movement had blossomed into an aggressive anti-alcohol campaign. In the United States, a national Prohibition amendment was enacted and was not repealed until 1933.

Interestingly, in the early 1800s, President Thomas Jefferson, a keen wine lover, wrote the following:

I rejoice as a moralist at the prospect of a reduction of the duties on wine by our national legislature. It is an error to view a tax on that liquor as merely a tax on the rich. It is a prohibition of its use to the idling class of our citizens, and

Here's to a temperance supper With water in glasses tall, And coffee and tea to end with — And me not there at all!

79

a condemnation of them to the poison of whiskey, which is desolating their houses. No nation is drunken where wine is cheap; and none sober where the dearness of wine substitutes ardent spirits as the common beverage. It is, in truth, the only antidote to the bane of whiskey. Fix but the duty at the rate of other merchandise, and we can drink wine here as cheap as grog; and who will not prefer it? Its extended use will carry health and comfort to a much enlarged circle. Everyone in easy circumstances (as the bulk of our citizens are) will prefer it to the poison to which they are now driven by their government. And the treasury itself will find that a penny apiece from a dozen, is more than a groat from a single one. This reformation, however, will require time.

(To Jean Guillaume, Baron Hyde de Neuville, December 13, 1818)

On the lighter side, Prohibition *did* give rise to some memorable humor, such as W. C. Fields' famous quip, "What contemptible scoundrel stole the cork from my lunch?"

In Canada, in 1916, the premier of Ontario, Sir William Hearst, a keen Methodist and even keener prohibitionist, passed the Ontario Temperance Act. By the following year, all the provinces except

The Spirituality of Wine

Quebec followed suit. Quebec continued to hold out until 1919, and compromised then by banning hard liquor but not wine or beer. The 11 years that followed created a uniquely Canadian paradox.

Tony Aspler has noted that "prohibition, more than anything else, turned Canadians into a nation of wine-drinkers." Hard liquor and beer were banned. Wine remained the only alcoholic beverage that could be made and that could, under the right circumstances (for example, by pharmacies) be sold legally across the country. Wineries, often headed by immigrants from wine-making countries, "were started up in basements, at the back of grocery stores and in garages," Aspler says. Canadians consumed nearly 225,000 gallons of domestic wine during 1920–1921. Ten years later the amount was about 2,200,000 gallons for Ontario alone! Most of this was at maximum alcohol strength and was made from Concord grapes.

Without question, though, the best wine was still to come!

4

The Vine's Appeal

O, for a draught of vintage! that hath been
Cooled a long age in the deep-delved earth,
Tasting of Flora and the country green,
Dance, and Provençal song,
and sunburnt mirth!
O, for a beaker full of the warm South,
Full of the true, the blushful Hippocrene,
With beaded bubbles winking at the brim,
And purple-stained mouth.

JOHN KEATS
ODE TO A NIGHTINGALE

Few things in the whole panoply of nature hold more sensual appeal to the eye and to the touch than ripening bunches of grapes on the vine – especially in the early morning or just after a shower, when the plump globules are misted with fine droplets of dew. But wine itself appeals to each one of the senses and, at the same time, elevates the soul.

The almost infinite variety of wines – in the appeal to scent, taste, color, and feel on the palate – makes it one of the most exciting and most pleasurable surprises at any table.

SOUND

The soft extractive note of an aged cork
being withdrawn
has the true sound of a [person]
opening [his or her] heart.

WILLIAM S. BENWELL
JOURNEY TO WINE IN VICTORIA

For the ear, there is the quiet susurration of vine leaves in a gentle breeze, especially in the late haze of summer before the harvesting begins. There is the almost indescribably delicious sound of a popping cork, or the magical whisper as a fine wine is poured into a crystal glass. Can there be any sound more pleasurable to the human ear (and to the heart as well) than the clinking of glasses in the warm glow of fellowship before a meal. Listen to what happens even before a bottle of wine is opened and poured, or put on the table – conversation begins to flow and soon a happy buzz of talk, interrupted by joyous laughter, fills the room.

The clinking of goblets or glasses has been a popular practice for a great many years. In fact, the tradition may have begun during the Middle Ages, when the original intention of the clink was to produce

The Spirituality of Wine

a sound like a bell so as to banish the devil. Superstition held that the evil one could not abide the sound of the church-related tone. Another legend claims that clinking was meant to make liquid from one glass spill into the next, so that nobody would be tempted to poison a glass! Still others believed that all five senses should come into play with wine, to get the greatest pleasure from the drink. As George Sterling once wrote: "He who clinks his cup with mine, adds a glory to the wine."

How simple and frugal a thing is happiness; a glass of wine, a roast chestnut ...the sound of the sea.

NIKOS KAZANTZAKIS
(1883–1957)
ZORBA THE GREEK

85

SIGHT

*For in the hand of the Lord there is a cup
and the wine is red.*

PSALM 75:8

Wine appears to the eye in a kaleidoscopic way. Grape colors range from deep purple to the palest thin-spun gold. Wine in a sparkling crystal glass, or on the pour, pleasures the eye with a complete palette of hues. Held up to the light, it dazzles our sight with a riot of colors – brick-red, pale yellow, purple, ruby, tawny, and gris (very pale rose).

Few rural landscapes offer a more pleasing vista than sun-drenched rows of grapevines stretching up terraced hillsides in distant valleys, or huddling around old stone houses, castles, or monasteries. Or think of the ripe juicy roundness of the grapes themselves, misted with the dew

The Spirituality of Wine

of early morning; or of giant oak barrels or dusty bottles in dry cool caves and cellars.

SCENT

....they shall revive as the corn, and grow as the vine;
the scent thereof shall be as the wine of Lebanon.

HOSEA 14:7

The sense of smell, they say, stirs memories as nothing else can do — memories that include, if we are truly blessed, great wines; joyful, loving faces; and happy celebratory times. Certainly, the first sip tells the most important story of all. But taste depends to a great degree upon smell. And so the first inhalation of a wine's bouquet or scent marks its uniqueness and character with an indelible imprint. It is the prized promise of subtle delicacies to come.

The true center of wine appreciation resides in the upper nasal cavity, where in normal breathing the air never goes. But wine tasters know that the volatile aspects of wine rise as vapor when one inhales properly, and touch nerve centers that lie deep within the brain. Those nerve centers provide instant access to the brain's memory bank.

*From wine
what sudden
friendship springs!*
JOHN GAY
THE SQUIRE AND THE CUR

The wonderful thing about wine is that it is a living entity and that it goes on living once it is bottled. It takes time for the various elements to resolve themselves into an ultimately harmonious whole and to gain the distinct scent of maturity. Perhaps the only thing that can surpass the bouquet or "nose" of a fine wine is the language wine connoisseurs are apt to use to describe it – language overflowing with adjectives such as robust, light, sweet, fruity, floral, spicy, smoky, heady, and lively; and phrases describing a redolence of citrus, berries, pears, apples, vanilla, clove, and on and on…

The Spirituality of Wine

TOUCH

Quickly, bring me
a beaker of wine
so that I may whet my mind
and say something clever.
ARISTOPHANES (450–485 BCE)

The sense of touch is deeply involved in the entire process of wine-making and wine enjoyment. There is the sensual feel of the grapes themselves, the silky finesse of a fine bottle, especially when, as is increasingly prevalent, the label itself is a product of a professional artisan. There is the feel of the thin-stemmed glass as it is raised, and of course and quintessentially, the smooth and cooling wash over and under the tongue and palate at the first sip and swallow. It was the scintillating feel of a myriad of tiny bubbles bursting on his tongue that made Dom Perignon (1638–1714), who was blind and therefore couldn't see that the wine had bubbles, exclaim at his first sip of champagne, "Come quickly! I am tasting stars!"

Taste

It's a naïve domestic Burgundy without any breeding,
but I think you'll be amused by its presumption.

James Thurber

Cartoon caption, 1944

One not only drinks wine, one smells it, observes it,
tastes it, sips it and talks about it.

King Edward VII

Thurber was too shrewd a humorist not to see the extremes to which some wine enthusiasts go to describe their favorite wines. Be that as it may, taste is still the most important of wine's sensual lures. Taste has a deeply spiritual dimension, too.

The ultimate test of any spirituality is experience. Does it work? That's why the psalmist invites the reader to "taste and see that the Lord is good." Similarly, the ultimate invitation held out by any wine, however rare or renowned, is taste. Taste and see for yourself. Each person's palate is different, every vintage is different, and sometimes almost every bottle in that vintage differs by just a hint or trace. It is our sense of taste that leads to the greatest discrimination in the choosing

The Spirituality of Wine

and ranking of the greatest wines. It also leads to the most sensuous vocabulary used by the purveyors and connoisseurs of any agricultural product known to our species. Writing about a Niagara Chardonnay in *The Globe and Mail* (January 17, 2004), a wine columnist wrote that it was "seductively silky, delivering flavors of pear, apple and citrus, complemented by touches of smoky oak and vanilla." One is reminded of mystics and lovers who, like wine connoisseurs, eventually run out of language trying to express the ineffable.

For example, here's *The Toronto Star*'s wine critic Gordon Stimmell describing a particular Cabernet-Merlot "with spicy black cherry and licorice elegance"; or a Chardonnay Musque "with very polished aromas and flavors of pear, jasmine, and apple spice"; or another Chardonnay "with golden apple, coconut, and lemon-grass nuances." The whole vocabulary of wine evolution is lush, luxurious, head-spinning, and evocative of every sensory peak experience.

Charles Dickens, in this classic passage from his great novel *Bleak House*, illustrates the full range of the sensory appeal and delights of wine:

> Mr. Tulkinghorn sits at one of the open windows, enjoying
> a bottle of old port. Though a hard-grained man, close, dry,
> and silent, he can enjoy old wine with the best. He has a

priceless bin of port in some artful cellar under the Fields, which is one of his many secrets. When he dines alone in chambers, as he has dined today, and has his bit of fish and his steak or chicken brought in from the coffee-house, he descends with a candle to the echoing regions below the deserted mansion, and, heralded by the remote reverberation of thundering doors, comes gravely back, encircled by an earthy atmosphere and carrying a bottle from which he pours a radiant nectar, two score and ten years old, that blushes in the glass to find itself so famous, and fills the whole room with the fragrance of southern grapes.

It is because of its total sensory appeal that wine, more than any other natural substance, has lent itself in literature to an abundance of simile and metaphor and other elegant imagery. One of wine's great secrets is its power to lift and fire our imagination and understanding to new heights.

The Spirituality of Wine

THE AESTHETICS OF WINE

A thing of beauty is a joy forever:
Its loveliness increases; it will never
Pass into nothingness…

These immortal lines by the English poet John Keats (1795–1821) fittingly describe the artistic genius inspired by wine, as do those equally famous words in his unforgettable *Ode on a Grecian Urn* [or amphora]:

"Beauty is truth, truth beauty," – that is all
Ye know on earth, and all ye need to know.

Keats was highlighting for eternity what anyone who has ever visited the Greco-Roman wing of a top museum has discovered: that the ancients were not content simply to make functional containers for the highly esteemed gift of wine; they had their imaginations fired to even greater heights of beauty in design, and particularly in the way the amphorae or jars were adorned and decorated. From the pottery of classical Greece alone you can see almost every aspect of daily life depicted so gracefully and vividly that the whole long-ago world comes vibrantly alive.

Clearly, the aesthetics – the impulse of wine to the appreciation of beauty – has fostered and given rise to some of the greatest art and poetry in human culture all down the ages. That's partly why wine adds such grace and beauty to our lives. It floods our sensibilities with fresh delight in all that is best in human relationships and strivings. For this reason, it has come to be identified with fullness of life. Thus, wine radiates by substance and by implication our highest spiritual values. The aim of all religions and of all spiritualities, whether religiously based or not, is the richest possible experience of creation and of human life. Or as St. Irenaeus put it, "The glory of God is [humanity] fully alive!"

What wond'rous life is this I lead!
Ripe apples drop about my head;
The luscious clusters of the vine
Upon my mouth do crush their wine.
ANDREW MARVELL

5

The Healthful Blessings of the Grape

*Wine nourishes, refreshes and cheers.
Wine is the foremost of medicines…
wherever wine is lacking,
medicines become necessary.*
THE TALMUD

André Simon, noted wine expert and editor of the authoritative tome *Wines of the World*, writes in his introduction, "Joy and health are the gifts of wine, and they are priceless."

> *I have lived temperately, eating little animal food. Vegetables constitute my principal diet. I double, however, the doctor's glass and a half of wine, and even treble it with a friend.*
>
> THOMAS JEFFERSON,
> 1743–1826

My own background, however, held a very different view. My parents adhered to a strict, religion-based opposition to all forms of alcohol consumption. Both parents were teetotalers as a result of their early upbringing in the North of Ireland, where every person professing to be an evangelical Christian was expected to – and did – sign a temperance pledge of total abstinence. The Gospel Hall we attended in my childhood in Toronto used unfermented grape juice and not wine for the "Lord's Supper," as the sacrament of Holy Communion was known there.

Imagine, then, my surprise one day, many years later, as an undergraduate at Oriel College, Oxford, when I sat down with my philosophy don for my weekly tutorial and was told he had a piece of news to announce. I had never before seen him so animated and pleased. Richard Robinson, an authority on Plato, was a tallish, sallow-complexioned man who rarely smiled. "Harpur, happy people depress me," he had announced on one occasion, after coming in from the High Street where he had observed students in the coffee houses laughing and generally carrying on.

So I awaited his announcement with a feeling of wondering anticipation. He said, "I've made an important decision today that I must share." Then he blurted out, "I've resolved to have a glass of wine with lunch and dinner every day from today until the end of my life." I don't know what I expected, but I have never forgotten that moment.

That incident, now 50 years in the past, was etched on my memory by the events that followed. Robinson, who lived outside of the college, eventually retired at age 65. He continued, however, to dine and share a glass with the other Fellows at Oriel once a week or so until he was well past 90. According to reports published in the Oriel College Record, he remained active and brilliantly lucid until the very end of his life in 1996 at the age of 94.

I know this is only "anecdotal evidence" of the benefit of drinking wine, and of itself proves nothing. But had you known the man as well as I managed to get to know him, you too would be impressed. Outwardly, he did not seem to be what the famous Canadian doctor Sir William Osler was fond of calling "a strong organism."

> *If penicillin can cure those that are ill, Spanish sherry can bring the dead back to life.*
> SIR ALEXANDER FLEMING, 1881–1955

Better to pay the tavernkeeper than the druggist.
SPANISH PROVERB

The Spirituality of Wine

The Spirituality of Wine

From the medical tablets and papyri of ancient Sumer and Egypt thousands of years ago; to the "Father of Medicine," Hippocrates (c. 450 BCE); to the Bible; to modern medical studies – all consistently testify that wine is a health-enhancing blessing for most people, always, of course, provided it is taken wisely and moderately. Hippocrates, for example, recommended specific wines to purge fever, and to disinfect and dress wounds; other wines he said, could be used as diuretics, or as nutritional supplements.

One centuries-old reason why wine played so central a part in medicine, right up to the 18th century, was because of the inferior quality of drinking water before the advent of filtration and chlorination. Louis Pasteur, who became professor of chemistry and microbiology at the Sorbonne in 1867, said, "Wine is the most healthful and hygienic form of beverage."

You don't have to be a doctor to know that, in moderate amounts, wine works as a natural, mild tranquilizer, able to reduce anxiety and tension, and to induce a lighter spirit; and that it can also aid digestion and help one's energy flow.

Wine was created, from the beginning, to make [us] joyful, and not to make [us] drunk. Wine drunk with moderation is the joy of the soul and the heart.

Ecclesiasticus (Sirach) 31:27ff

THE CONTEMPORARY EVIDENCE

Ever since the well-publicized "Framington Heart Study" done in the 1970s, which showed that moderate drinkers had 50 percent fewer deaths from coronary disease than total abstainers or abusive drinkers, there has been a deluge of scientific studies examining the relation between moderate alcohol consumption, especially red wine, and health in general. What really sped up the tempo and the intensity of the research was the Sunday, November 17, 1991, edition of the CBS news program *60 Minutes*, which announced to the world what has come to be known as The French Paradox. The French Paradox refers to the apparently contradictory situation that exists, especially in southwestern France, where people consume large amounts of saturated fats – rich cheeses and patés – smoke cigarettes made of strong tobacco (Gauloises), and exercise very little, and yet, nevertheless, suffer one of the lowest rates of heart attack in the world. The researchers suggested that the compensating factor was that the French drink red wine at most meals. In the United States and Canada, sales of red wine instantly rocketed up by 40 percent and remained steady for a full year following.

Sergé Rénaud, the original "French Paradox" researcher, later went on to further research aided by colleagues from the University of Bordeaux. His findings were published in the March 1998 issue of

The Spirituality of Wine

Epidemiology. A large study he made of middle-aged men in France found that a moderate daily amount of red wine was associated with a 35 percent reduction in deaths from cardiovascular diseases, a 30 percent drop in deaths from all causes, and an 18–24 percent reduction in deaths from cancer. Many more similar projects with similar results have followed. As yet there are far too many variables in these and in the scores of other studies done since – in countries around the world, from Australia to China – to say definitively that the matter has now been "proven" beyond any shadow of doubt.

But the theory is that the flavonoids or catechins involved – resveratrol, quercetin, epicatechin – plus the tannins, acid, and alcohol, combine to boost the immune system, block some forms of cancer formation, reduce low density cholesterol (LDL), and fight platelet blockage of arteries. Red wine has been singled out because it contains the highest amount of polyphenols or antioxidants of all alcoholic beverages. These mop up free radicals and help prevent atherosclerosis, or hardening of the arteries. However, wine experts at the University of Montpelier in France have recently produced a Chardonnay, called Paradox Blanc, which they now claim has the same benefits as red wine. Other countries are quickly following this lead.

In short, study after study has concluded that most healthy people who drink wine regularly and moderately live longer. My old Oriel tutor may well have had more going for him than his genetic inheritance. According to present information, the single group exception whose members should *not* consume alcohol in any form, is pre-menopausal women whose family history includes breast cancer. Overall, the key always is moderation. Overindulgence is more harmful than abstinence.

A single glass of champagne
imparts a feeling of exhilaration.
The nerves are braced; the imagination is stirred,
the wits become more nimble.
A bottle produces the contrary effect.
Excess causes a comatose insensibility.
WINSTON CHURCHILL

Winston Churchill knew better than most the truth of which he spoke. In his obituary notice in *The New York Times*, his great fondness for drink of all kinds was described. He drank wine for breakfast when it pleased him to do so, and champagne and brandy and whisky through

The Spirituality of Wine

the rest of the day. He smoked cigars continually. He never exercised and yet seemed to exude vigor and health. He died at 91. It all finally caught up to him!

Wine sloweth age, it strengtheneth youth,
it helpeth digestion, it abandoneth melancholie,
it relisheth the heart, it lighteneth the mind,
it quickeneth the spirits, it keepeth and preserveth
the head from whirling, the eyes from dazzling,
the tongue from lisping, the mouth from snaffling,
the teeth from chattering, and the throat from rattling;
it keepeth the stomach from wambling,
the heart from swelling, the hands from shivering,
the sinews from shrinking, the veins from crumbling,
the bones from aching, and the marrow from soaking.

ANONYMOUS, 13TH CENTURY

A WINE LOVER'S DIARY

The Spirituality of Wine

The Spirituality of Wine

The old, classical motto for wholeness was *mens sana in corpore sano* – a healthy mind in a sound or healthy body. But as I have pointed out in my book *Finding the Still Point*, the new paradigm for human holistic well-being is that of a single, integrated organism made up of body, mind, *and spirit*. These three have been "joined together by God" or the Ground of the universe, and are only sundered apart to our serious loss. That which enriches and inspires the spirit uplifts the whole person. No wonder wine's role in humanity's religious and spiritual quest has been so large; it lends itself powerfully to the living of a balanced and happy life.

6

The Bible
Is Filled with Wine

And Melchizedek king of Salem
brought forth bread and wine:
and he was the priest of the most high God.

Genesis 14:18 (KJV)

And Noah he often said to his wife
when he sat down to dine,
"I don't care where the water goes if it
doesn't get into the wine!"

G. K. Chesterton (1874–1936)

The Spirituality of Wine

The Spirituality of Wine

By far the greatest testimony to the antiquity and centrality of wine and wine-making for early civilization comes from the Bible. The Bible is literally drenched in wine! No single plant or product is mentioned more frequently in the 66 books that make up the Bible than the vine and its fruit. In all, there are over 200 references to wine itself. It is mentioned 21 times in the Book of Isaiah alone; 14 times in Jeremiah; 12 in times Deuteronomy; 11 times in Proverbs, 8 times in Daniel, and 7 times in Revelation. It is cited, in fact, in almost every book of the Bible. It is part of the vision of the Messianic banquet and feasting in the age to come; it is central to the Last Supper; it is at the cross in the form of a wine vinegar offered to the dying Jesus; and it is present at the end of the age in the imagery of judgment in the Book of Revelation.

In the Bible, wine is the pivotal focus of hospitality. Together with corn or wheat, it is a staple of life for the people of God, and a vital expression of all their joy and celebration. "And they of Ephraim shall be like a mighty man and their heart shall rejoice as through wine…" says the prophet Zechariah (7:10, KJV). In the highly erotic poetry of the Song of Solomon, only sensuous romantic love is better than wine: "How sweet is your love…my bride! How much better is your love than wine!" (4:10).

[God gives] wine to gladden the human, oil to make the face shine, and bread to strengthen the human heart.

PSALM 104:15

109

The Bible recognizes the risks of drinking excess wine and other strong drink, to be sure. It warns against this with blunt honesty. But the overall approach is overwhelmingly positive and affirmative. Wine symbolizes as nothing else does the fully civilized and blessed human life.

In all of this, the biblical authors, over the span of centuries, were reflecting and inheriting the rich wine culture of the entire Mediterranean basin and hinterland. The oldest known laws, Hammurabi's Code (from Babylon, c. 1771 BCE), regulated drinking houses. Pre-biblical cuneiform records from Ugarit, in ancient northern Canaan (Palestine), reveal abundant references to the household and religious uses of wine. Egyptian doctors, and the Sumerians before them, included beer or wine in a significant percentage of all prescriptions, according to medical papyri and cuneiform tablets. This reminds us of the renowned New Testament story of the Good Samaritan, who gave curbside first-aid to a stranger who had been mugged by thieves on the Jericho to Jerusalem road. He treated the man's wounds, "pouring in oil and wine" – oil to soothe, and wine as an antiseptic. This type of "medical" usage is paralleled in Paul's advice to his youthful Christian helper, Timothy, when he writes, "take a little wine for the sake of your stomach and your frequent ailments" (1 Timothy 5:23). The psalmist also knew nearly three millennia ago what modern doctors have been confirming today – that for many, the moderate drinking of wine can act as a medicine for body and mind.

The very first mention of the institutional use of flour and wine in the Bible comes in 1 Chronicles 9:29: "Some of them [Levites or priests] also were appointed to oversee the vessels, and all the instruments of the sanctuary, and the fine flour, and the wine, and the oil, and the frankincense, and the spices" (KJV).

A Noteworthy Biblical Connection

The wine bottles of today date back only about 300 years. They come, particularly champagne bottles, in a variety of sizes. Remarkably, all of the larger ones have biblical names: the largest of all, a Nebuchadnezzar, holds about 100 glasses or roughly 20 times the amount of the usual 750 ml bottle. The name is from Nebuchadnezzar, King of Babylon (c. 604–561 BCE) who appears in several Old Testament books, especially Daniel. A Balthazar (traditionally the name of one of the Wise Men) holds 80 glasses; a Salmanazar (after a king of Assyria) contains 60 glasses; a Methuselah (the oldest man in the Bible) contains 40; a Rehoboam (after a King of Israel) holds 30; a Jeroboam (also a King of Israel) holds 20; a simple magnum holds 10; a litre bottle about six and a half; and a split, the smallest, holds about 1.5 glasses.

111

Wine as a Gift of Good Will

Today we have a custom of taking along a bottle of wine when we're invited to someone's house for dinner. Here's the first known instance of it that practice: "Jesse [David's father] took a donkey loaded with bread, a skin of wine, and a kid, and sent them by his son David to Saul" (1 Samuel 16:20). Jesse was keen to make a good initial impression for the young man, but it was a common courtesy and an offer of warm friendship then as it is today.

The Spirituality of Wine

ABUNDANCE AND BLESSING

Plenteous wine in Judaism is invariably a sign of blessing: "Then your barns will be filled with plenty, and your vats burst out with new wine" (Proverbs 3:10).

As Jacob (Israel) blesses his son Judah in Genesis 49:11, his vision of total bliss for him is that he will "bind his foal unto the vine, and his ass's colt unto the choice vine; he washes his garments in wine, and his clothes in the blood of grapes…"

The idea that wine blesses and cheers both God and humanity runs throughout scripture: "Then the trees said to the vine, 'You come and reign over us.' But the vine said to them, 'Shall I stop producing my wine that cheers gods and mortals and go to sway over the trees?'" (Judges 9:12–13).

In the end, it never left its wine but was promoted over the other trees anyway! It may well have been "the tree of life" in the story of the Garden of Eden in Genesis, and quite likely was the tree referred to "whose leaves are for the healing of the nations" in Revelation 22:2.

When Isaac blessed Jacob he said, "May God give you of the dew of heaven,…and plenty of grain and wine"(Genesis 27:28). From the instructions on what is to be given to the priests of the

Lord: "All the best of the oil and all the best of the wine and of the grain…"(Numbers 18:12).

Moses pronounces God's blessing: "[God] will love you, and bless you, and multiply you; [God] will also bless … the fruit of your ground, your grain and your wine and your oil…" (Deuteronomy 7:13).

Several passages also make it plain that an extraordinary *surplus* of wine is taken as nothing less than a vivid token of the coming of the Messianic Age: "The time is surely coming, says the Lord, when… the mountains shall drip sweet wine, and all the hills shall flow with it" (Amos 9:13).

FOR GOOD CHEER

Go, eat your bread with enjoyment,
and drink your wine with a merry heart.
ECCLESIASTES 9:17

Give strong drink to one who is perishing,
and wine to those in bitter distress.
PROVERBS 31:6

But wine is always about sharing and caring too. In Leviticus 19:10, explicit instructions are given not to "glean the vineyard," i.e., strip it wholly bare. A small surplus must be left "for the poor and stranger." This may not be practical today, but it is a strong reminder that enjoying wine's bounty to the full means accepting a social responsibility for the disadvantaged and the weak among us.

HOPE

The highest vision of peace any prophet or historian could express is colorfully portrayed in this poetic, ever romantic hope: "During Solomon's lifetime Judah and Israel lived in safety, from Dan even to Beersheba, all of them under their vines and fig trees" (1 Kings 4:25). This note of each person eating and drinking from his or her own vine stands out like a constant refrain in the Hebrew Bible. It's idyllic. It is, at the same time, a vivid image of inner peace, contentment, and joy of spirit.

The Spirituality of Wine

The Spirituality of Wine

JUDGMENT

Because of wine's enormous importance in day-to-day life in ancient Judaism – both in secular and religious settings – and because of its symbolic significance as a sign of spiritual blessing, naturally there was a more shadow side as well. If *abundance* of wine signifies God's pleasure, then a blight on the vines or a *dearth* of wine represents the theme of judgment.

In Job 15:33 we read, "They will shake off their unripe grape, like the vine, and cast off their blossoms, like the olive tree."

"The wine dries up, the vine languishes, all the merry-hearted sigh" (Isaiah 24:7).

Jeremiah thunders, "I will make an end of them, says the Lord. There are no grapes on the vine, nor figs on the fig tree, even the leaves are withered…" (Jeremiah 8:13). And again: "Thus says the Lord of Hosts: Glean thoroughly as a vine the remnant of Israel; like a grape-gatherer, pass your hand again over its baskets" (Jeremiah 6:9).

Ezekiel, however, is not to be outdone. He knows that the vine often stands as a symbol of God's own people: "O mortal, how does the wood of the vine surpass all other wood – the vine branch that is among the trees of the forest?…Therefore thus says the Lord God: Like the wood of the vine among the trees of the forest, which I have given to the fire for fuel, so I will give up the inhabitants of Jerusalem" (15:2, 6).

Joel will have the last word on this darker theme: "For a nation has invaded my land…It has laid waste my vines, and splintered my fig trees…the vine withers, the fig tree droops. Pomegranate, palm and apple – all the trees of the field are dried up; surely, joy withers away among the people" (1:6–7, 12).

LOVELY IMAGERY

Some of the most mystically beautiful speech in any literature is entwined with vineyards, grapes, and wine, in the pages of the Bible. Listen to these vivid phrases: "Thou hast made us drink the wine of astonishment"(Psalm 60:3, KJV). Or, "they eat the bread of wickedness and drink the wine of violence" (Proverbs 4:17). It is moving to read the following, from the lovesick writer of the Song of Songs: "I went down to the nut orchard, to look at the blossoms of the valley, to see whether the vines had budded, whether the pomegranates were in bloom" (Proverbs 6:11).

The psalmist rhapsodizes, "Your wife will be like a fruitful vine within your house; your children will be like olive shoots around your table" (Psalm 128:3).

Ezekiel sings, "Your mother was like a vine in a vineyard transplanted by the water, fruitful and full of branches from abundant water" (19:10).

So prevalent is wine imagery in the minds of the biblical authors that even some of the great dreams recorded in holy writ glow with the symbolic richness of grape, vine, and wine archetypes. Take, for example, the well-known story of Joseph, who was asked while in an Egyptian prison to interpret the dream of the Pharaoh's chief butler: "So the chief cupbearer told his dream to Joseph, and said to him, 'In my dream there was a vine before me, and on the vine there were three branches. As soon as it budded, its blossoms came out and the clusters ripened into grapes'" (Genesis 40:9–10).

Of course, wine imagery is not unique to the Bible. The poetry in the *Rubaiyat of Omar Khayyam* is replete with mystical wine symbolism. We think at once of those familiar lines from verse 11:

> *Here with a loaf of bread beneath the bough,*
> *A flask of wine, A book of verse – and thou*
> *Beside me singing in the wilderness –*
> *And wilderness is paradise enow!*

One of the lesser-known lines is even more lovely and revelatory of the author's deep spirituality: "Man is a cup, his soul the wine therein…."

Perhaps the most gripping and potent imagery of all is contained in these lines which compare the gospel, or good news, with the potential explosiveness of new wine: "Neither is new wine put into old wineskins; otherwise, the skins burst, and the wine is spilled, and the skins are destroyed; but new wine is put into fresh wineskins, and so both are preserved" (Matthew 9:17).

Quite honestly, I have taught and studied the Bible in depth throughout all of my adult life, but never, until embarking upon the special research required for this book, have I fully realized the magnitude and range of vine and wine imagery – and its special symbolism – contained in these sacred texts. There is a vast richness and glory here to be savored.

7

Celebrating Life

Wine is…a beverage that goes through a "life cycle"
that closely resembles that of humans'
fresh and untamed in youth, mellowing to maturity
in mid-cycle, and continuing to show…signs of its best
qualities even as it ages into final dissolution.
It is thus easy to see why wine has historically been
associated with the celebration of life and used in
ceremonies commemorating significant rites of passage.

ROBERT C. FULLER

RELIGION AND WINE

CELEBRATING SIGNIFICANT MOMENTS

The wine festivals we know today, and that grow in number year by year, have their origins many millennia in the past. There's a powerful force behind this phenomenon. The rituals of our life cycle are not just key moments in the making of our lives, they are our vital link to others and to all the generations past. They forge our spiritual heritage by taking what seems "ordinary" or even "routine" on the surface, and elevating it into a special, never-to-be-forgotten moment. The reason our ancient ancestors celebrated every stage in the making of wine was that they saw in every step a mirror of their own lives. The analogy ran at several levels, from the purely social to the inner development of their unique spiritual lives.

Rituals of all kinds play a central role in the revitalization of social structures and the establishment and reinforcement of genuine community. They supply a framework for and an energizing of interpersonal relationships. They bring people together beyond the routines of their daily lives and shed a grace and beauty that radiates with an appreciation of the more spiritual dimensions of our common life.

Rituals *do* matter, then, whether it's an old family custom, or how a bottle of wine is presented, uncorked, allowed to breathe, held to the light for color, swirled in the glass and sniffed for bouquet, and finally savored

The Spirituality of Wine

over tongue and palate. And from the very beginning, at births, initiation ceremonies, comings of age, religious worship, joyous anniversaries, and even at the moment of death, wine has always been there. It is more than a faithful companion to the human journey; its mystic, transformative secrets add an uplifting ferment to enhance it all.

The Magic of Toasts

Let us make our glasses kiss;
Let us quench the sorrow cinders.
RALPH WALDO EMERSON, 1851
THE PERSIAN OF HAFIZ

Here's to us all! God bless us every one!
CHARLES DICKENS, *A CHRISTMAS CAROL*

A man will be eloquent if you give him good wine.
RALPH WALDO EMERSON

Nobody can say with absolute certainty when or where the practice started of making the celebration of special events, special relationships, and special seasons of the year, a time for drinking toasts. But the tradition of toasting the good health, success, or shared humanity of outstanding figures (such as the Queen or other head of state) and of those close to us (relatives, friends, colleagues) is very ancient indeed. And its central feature is wine.

There was undoubtedly toasting in the Bible's accounts of great banquets, such as the one presided over by Belshazzar, son of King Nebuchadnezzar of Babylon, when he "made a great festival for a thousand of his lords, and he was drinking wine in the presence of the thousand" (Daniel 5:1). (Belshazzar was celebrating his father's rape of the treasures

The Spirituality of Wine

of the Jewish temple in Jerusalem.) It is also certain that toasts are implied in the wedding story in John's gospel, where water was turned into wine and the startled host found he was serving "the best wine" last.

The ancient Egyptians, Chaldeans, and Babylonians all drank plenteous toasts. The evidence is clear, as well, that the Greeks and the Romans drank sips of wine as toasts, to express their deepest feelings of love, friendship, joy, hope, and concern for the common good of all. Homer, in his great epic *The Odyssey*, tells how Ulysses drank to the health of Achilles. Very much later, the character Falstaff, when requesting a jug of wine in Shakespeare's *The Merry Wives of Windsor*, said, "Put toast in it."

The source of this custom and the name have varied explanations. Drinking wine from a large common jar or wineskin was a pledge of trust that the wine had not been poisoned, some experts say. But the deep symbolism of binding friendships and loyalties by sharing in the one wine and by holding high the glasses – signifying both elevation of mood and longings for a more expansive "higher" life – had, of course, deeply spiritual connections. People were extending into all aspects of daily life – from marriage, to personal achievements, to death itself – the sacred meanings of wine at the core of their communal religious life. The central thrust of toasting is to lift up a special moment, bathe it in the

To wine, it improves with age: The older I get, the more I like it.

Give me wine to wash me clean Of the weather-stains of cares.
RALPH WALDO EMERSON
THE PERSIAN

May you always work like you don't need money; May you always love like you've never been hurt; And may you always dance like there's nobody watching.

light of a common intention, and thus make it forever memorable.

Few people notice it, because it doesn't leap out at you as formal religious language would. But, if you listen closely, many toasts are in reality an affirmative yet non-pious kind of prayer. Take Tiny Tim's toast, from Charles Dickens' *A Christmas Carol*. It's an invocation of God's blessing upon everyone in the room. When I was a student at Oxford, I noticed that the toast to the Queen was almost always accompanied by the words, "God bless her." Drinking a toast of wine to someone's good health is a spiritual act insofar as it asks the energies and Mind of the universe to prosper and keep safe the person being toasted. A toast to the success of any enterprise, from a marriage to the launching of a ship, is a way of asking divine providence to shine on all concerned. Sometimes, depending on the circumstances and the wisdom and grace of the one proposing the toast, the implicit prayer can carry a deep sense of balance and admonition.

Here, for example, is one such toast from the poet Ogden Nash:

To wine, may those who use it never abuse it.

Then here's to the heartening wassail,
Wherever good fellows are found;
Be its master instead of its vassal,
and order the glasses around.

The Spirituality of Wine

Some toasts, of course, are more frivolous!

In all this world, why I do think
There are four reasons why we drink:
Good friends,
Good wine,
Lest we be dry,
And any other reason why!
FAMOUS QUOTES

Merry met, and
merry part
I drink to you
with all my heart.

The word "toast," from the Latin *tostus,* meaning parched or roasted, came, it is believed, from the Greco-Roman practice of placing a square of spiced, burned bread or toast in a cup of wine. None of the ancient wines were as controlled and refined in their production as today's vintages, by a long way. Scholars speculate, however, that excessive acidity or other "off" features could have been at least partially filtered and improved by the charcoal and the spice.

No matter, really. The point is that toasting is here to stay and that it can be a source of goodwill and social improvement that bonds and eases the welding together of groups small and large. I particularly like the Jewish toast *l'Chaim!* – "to life!" But we each have our favorites,

When wine
enlivens the heart
May friendship
surround the
table.

*Feasts are made
for laughter;
wine
gladdens life…*
ECCLESIASTES 10:19

depending on the circumstances and the mood. The best toasts are always brief, and from the heart or spirit of the one making the toast. What's important is that a felicitous toast can transform an ordinary moment into something rare and beautiful, and thus enhance the fleeting with a glimpse of the eternal. Toasts are always more than a hope for the future. They're an illumination of the power of the "now."

The Spirituality of Wine

FOOD AND WINE...

In Europe we thought of wine as something
as healthy and normal as food
and also a great giver of happiness
and well-being and delight.
Drinking wine was not a snobbism nor
a sign of sophistication nor a cult;
it was as natural as eating and to me as necessary.

ERNEST HEMINGWAY, *A Moveable Feast*

I was enjoying myself...I had taken two finger-bowls of champagne, and the scene had changed before my eyes into something significant, elemental and profound.

F. SCOTT FITZGERALD

Wine has always been a constant companion of feasting and the enjoyment of food both simple and gourmet, ever since the discovery of the mystery of fermentation was made 10,000 or so years ago. Food and wine go together as closely as body and soul. The unvarnished truth is that our ancestors discovered what all wine-lovers know today: nothing adds more to the joyous appreciation of wholesome, delectable dishes than the right wine, be it a Cabernet, Pinot Noir, Chardonnay, Riesling, or any one of a thousand different varieties and labels. No celebration, no special meal, no banquet to mark some honor or achievement is truly complete without it.

…AND SPRINGTIME CELEBRATIONS

Think of it: In springtime in the wine-growing regions of the world, "budbreak," the very first sign of the new season's grape crop, is always an occasion of celebration. One front-page ad in a local paper, placed by a Napa Valley wine store, calls everyone to join in the festival: "Budbreak is here. Let's count our blessings and lift our glasses to a new season of cheer!" Inside the paper, various delicacies, recipes to accompany specific wines, and complete meals are detailed and illustrated in such a way as to make one's mouth water. Good food and good wine make for a full heart and a contented mind.

The Spirituality of Wine

THE WORLD ATLAS OF WINE

In springtime, the Jewish community prepares its special foods and lays in a store of wine for celebrating not just the renewal and bursting forth of new life, but the various levels of spiritual liberation symbolized by Passover. Worshippers reflect upon, challenge, and release themselves from slavery of all kinds – to selfishness, to stress, to conventional wisdom, or to surface social values rather than one's own deep, inner intuitions and the higher self. The various tastes, from bitter herbs to sweet wines, reflect the multi-textured nature of our daily lives. Gratitude wells up to God for blessings of the past, and hoped for in the future. Family ties mellow in the glow of warmth that surrounds everything.

Similarly, the Christian community glories in the analogy between the rebirth of nature and the gospel story of the Resurrection hope. Death has given way to life. There is a sense and an experience of reawakening contact, not just with the natural world in its springing forth to new life, but with the Source and Author of the whole of creation. The Easter communion, with its sacramental bread and wine, is perfectly mirrored and reinforced in the Easter meal that follows. Each celebration is sacramental in its own way and has the ability to transform and spiritually empower all who take part. Every Sunday

A meal without wine is a stingy meal.
SPANISH PROVERB

135

following, throughout the year, is traditionally called "a little Easter."

Of course, one must not forget the deep springtime rituals and spirituality of those who belong to no traditional faith community, or who cannot accept a transcendent/immanent spiritual Source for all things, but who celebrate the spring solstice for its own sake, or out of deep commitment to and love for the whole of nature's wonders. These celebrations enhance our common humanity and the inner being of those who participate in them. The inextricable bond between food and wine as celebration and symbol of the joy of being alive with one another, at an exceptionally special time of year, unites us all as members of one cosmic family.

THANKSGIVING FOR ABUNDANCE

Meister Eckhart, the medieval mystic whose creation-based spirituality is so relevant and much-admired today, once wrote that to say "thanks" to God was the supreme, and all-sufficient prayer. It was his way of highlighting the significance, to the whole of one's spiritual life, of an attitude of gratitude – gratitude, once we stop to reflect, for the abundance of riches surrounding even the poorest of us. The occasions for celebration we've just looked at are also moments of profound thankfulness. Any true celebration is marked by an awareness – whether

The Spirituality of Wine

it is explicitly verbalized or not – that we are all debtors to nature's bounty, to human skills used in synergy with creation's gifts, and to each other. Just as the priest says a prayer of thanksgiving over the elements of bread and wine for the Eucharist, and as the presiding figure at a Seder supper offers thanks to God over the unleavened *matzoh* bread and the cup, so every dinner or meal where wine is present is its own blessing, of and for the abundance of the Earth.

Sometimes some of the wine is deliberately spilled by overfilling a glass. In the Hebrew Bible, we are told the priests in ancient times often poured wine on the altar to consecrate it, but also to show the divine bounty. All of this deeply symbolizes God's gift of abundance. As the psalmist says: "You anoint my head with oil; my cup overflows." It helps to see every opening of a bottle of wine and its first outpouring at any meal as a libation or drink-offering, as a celebration of all we've experienced and of the Source of all Being's constant goodness towards us. There is nothing quite so powerfully restorative, especially when stresses come and difficulties must be solved or endured, as the remembrance of divine goodness and of the abundance of grace and mercy we've received in the past. When we count our blessings, we are sometimes – perhaps often – surprised "at what the Lord has done!" to quote the old hymn. It reminds us of what God still can do. And so it brings hope.

Happiness is a wine of rarest vintage,
(and [only] seems insipid to a vulgar taste).
LOGAN PEARSALL SMITH, 1865–1946

MINDFULNESS

A bottle of good wine, like a good act,
shines ever in the retrospect.
ROBERT LOUIS STEVENSON
THE SILVERADO SQUATTERS

One of the most powerful resources that belongs to all spiritual traditions, and which in our time has been brought back to our attention in a convincing fashion by Eastern religions, is the art of *mindfulness*. Put quite simply, mindfulness means learning how to slow down, how to live wholly in – and to savor to its fullness – every moment of every day. Put another way, it is the art of being awake, of being totally aware, of living in the now. Mindfulness is the true secret of celebrating life, and it is also, in large measure, precisely what the fascination with wine is all about. Sharing a bottle of wine, assessing its qualities, appreciating its delicate bouquet, conversing over its origin – these things immediately banish all our scattered thoughts and cares, put the brakes on our stressed-out

The Spirituality of Wine

rushing about, and focus us in the glory and glow of the sacred present. Wine is the perfect catalyst for mindfulness and hence is a spiritually healing balm for tattered souls today. In this spirit, to paraphrase the words of William Morris, let us drink to this moment and to the days that are – as well as to those that will be.

INSPIRATION AND SURPRISE

Fill every glass,
For wine inspires us,
And fires us
With courage, love and joy…
JOHN GAY, 1685–1732

C. S. Lewis, the well-known Oxford don and professor of English who, though he died in 1963, still is widely read today, once wrote a book called *Surprised by Joy*. It told the story of his early life and of how he turned from atheism to a living faith in God. Our spirituality, whether faith-based or not, is the side of our lives that carries our deepest meanings and values, and is full of continual surprises – new insights, new friends, new experiences, new visions of our true selves and those of others. It is partly the romance and adventure of ever facing the unknown. As the great Canadian novelist Robertson Davies once told me in an interview, "My reason for getting up each morning is that I simply can't wait to see what's going to happen next!"

The enjoyment of wine is just like that. Even with a wine that's tried and true, an old favorite, there's always a moment of anticipation at the popping of the cork, followed by the surprise of the first sniff and telling taste. Each new bottle is an opportunity for a unique, deeply shared moment of pleasure – not just sensual pleasure, but one which touches mind and heart with warmth and delight. False inhibitions based on nameless anxieties and fears or on social unease are released and fall away. We begin to relax so our true inner light can shine forth. Our imagination is filled with fresh possibilities and new horizons.

The Spirituality of Wine

WINE AND ROMANTIC LOVE

*Wine, to strengthen friendship and
light the flame of love.*
ANONYMOUS

The deep connection between wine and romantic, erotic love is interwoven inextricably into the relations between the sexes and has far more to do with the life of the spirit than theologians have sometimes wished to admit. Yet as I mention in the preface to *The Divine Lover*, a small book of love poems to my wife, it is precisely because of the power of romantic love to take us out of ourselves; to transcend our ordinary feelings and attitudes, that the great mystics have always seen it as a metaphor of God's love of human souls. Unfortunately, the wish of many people within traditional religion to spiritualize everything, to make it less grounded in the earthiness of actual experience – particularly anything remotely connected with the body, sexuality, or eroticism – has minimized our awareness of the Divine Presence in and around the actual experience of being "in love" itself.

Being "in love" takes us to new levels of consciousness and so does the controlled, moderate use of wine. Both help us to feel and know the

*Wine prepares
the heart
for love,
Unless you take
too much.*
OVID
THE ART OF LOVE

141

"I was putting forward the notion," Denis went on, "that the effects of love were often similar to the effects of wine, that Eros could intoxicate as well as Bacchus…"

FROM CROME YELLOW, ALDOUS HUXLEY

energizing, creative presence of God. Sharing a carafe or bottle of wine with the person you deeply love and who just as deeply loves you is one of the greatest joys we may know. We are all potential mystics and to those open to it such experiences can help us taste the very elixir of life itself.

The Song of Solomon, or Song of Songs, is the most sensuous, erotically charged book of the Bible. The language is earthy, yet the poetry divine, and the themes are redolent of all the rich enticements of the natural world. But typically, too many Jewish and Christian scholars have tried to see it purely as a coded or symbolic expression of God's love. *The Oxford Dictionary of the Christian Church* primly comments, "Indeed apart from such an interpretation it would be hard to justify its inclusion in the Biblical Canon."

In reality, this ode to love, for the first time in great literature, makes a vineyard a wonderful place of romance and of sensual love. With high poetry it reads, "My beloved is to me a bundle of myrrh that lies between my breasts. My beloved is to me a cluster of henna blossoms in the vineyards of Engedi. Ah, you are beautiful, my love…" (Song of Songs 1:13–15).

The speaker at this point is a beautiful woman, "the keeper of the vineyards." And amidst the profusion of entrancing imagery – orchards of pomegranate and every other kind of "pleasant fruits"; and scents

Oh, may your breasts be like clusters of the vine, and the scent of your breath like apples, and your kisses like the best wine that goes down smoothly, gliding over lips and teeth.

SONG OF SOLOMON 7:9

such as frankincense, cinnamon, myrrh and aloes, all attended by the gurgling splash of "streams of living waters" – vines and grapes abound as metaphor as well as fact.

In hauntingly lovely, seductive tones, and after hinting her lover's face carries the scent of apples, the beautiful young woman says, "Let us go out early to the vineyards, and see whether the vines have budded, whether the grape blossoms have opened, and the pomegranates are in bloom. There will I give you my love"(Song of Songs 7:12).

Speaking of the little conflicts that sometimes result in foolish lovers' quarrels, the woman says, "Catch us the foxes [cares], the little foxes, that ruin the vineyards [of love] – for our vineyards are in blossom" (Song of Songs 2:15).

The male lover later replies: "How fair and pleasant you are, O loved one, delectable maiden!... your breasts be like clusters of the vine, and the scent of your breath like apples, and your kisses like the best wine that goes down smoothly, gliding over lips and teeth"(Song of Songs 7:6, 8–9).

In fact, when you follow the thread of this theme through the Bible, from the ubiquity of wine at all festive celebrations and feasts right through to the miracle of the wine at the wedding in Cana, you realize that the modern linking of wine with courtship and marriage is scriptural and spiritual throughout.

The Spirituality of Wine

FRIENDSHIP

Old wood to burn, old wine to drink, old friends to trust,
and old authors to read.
FRANCIS BACON

Do not abandon old friends,
for new ones cannot equal them.
A new friend is like new wine; when it has aged,
you can drink it with pleasure.
ECCLESIASTICUS (SIRACH) 9:10

Few things contribute more to our sense of belonging to the entire world than being able to choose a wine, say, from a certain cellar in northern Italy; or a specific vineyard in Bordeaux, France; or from a hillside or valley in sunny California, South Africa, Chilé, Australia, or Canada. Wine creates a global fellowship all its own, giving us one more reason to acknowledge the deeply related kinship of the human family.

On a more personal, individual level, some of the greatest writers and thinkers of all time have commented on the remarkable ability of wine to create and deepen one of the most priceless spiritual experiences known to any of us – that of deep and lasting friendships. Charles Dickens writes often on this theme, but here's one of his more colorful observations: "Fan the sinking flame of hilarity with the wing of friendship, and pass the rosy wine!"

Thomas Carlyle, a 19th-century historian, philosopher, and critic, once wrote that people who have some form of communication and little else can "eat together, and can still rise into some glow of brotherhood over food and wine." I think many of us have often experienced that.

Listen to the old Spanish proverb: "For a wine to taste like real wine, it has to be drunk with a friend." (El vino, para que sepa a vino, bebelo con un amigo.) This theme echoes down the ages to us in a tiny snippet of conversation from the famous fifth-century BCE Greek sculptor, Callimachus, who spoke of "laughter, at the right moment, over the wine."

The Roman poet, Ovid, explains part of the secret in *The Art of Love* (c. 8 CE): "Where there is plenty of wine, sorrow and worry take wing."

We catch it, too, in Tennyson's memorable and haunting lines, written almost two millennia later, about the growth of friendship "in after dinner talk, across the walnuts and wine." Tennyson was fond of wine and often spoke of its finer blandishments. In a note of invitation

...of this wine, if
of any other, may
be verified that
merry induction:
That good wine
makes good blood,
good blood
causeth
good humour,
good humours
cause
good thoughts,
good thoughts
bring forth
good works,
good works carry
a man to heaven,
ergo, good wine
carrieth a man
to heaven.

JAMES HOWELL, 1634

The Spirituality of Wine

he once sent to the distinguished cleric, the Reverend F. D. Maurice, he slyly observed, "You'll have no scandal while you dine, but honest talk and wholesome wine."

Most of us know the warm experience of taking along a bottle of wine to the home of a friend or couple who have invited us over for dinner. Something about it always evokes a sense of pleasure and anticipation. It's a kind of sacramental act, a way of sealing the bonds of friendship and of setting a harmonious mood. Sometimes they will open it and serve it before the meal; sometimes they will put it graciously on one side because they've already selected a special wine to go with the food they plan to serve. But however the occasion develops, offering a bottle of wine you have discussed and expressly chosen is an effective, though simple, mode of pursuing a deeper level of communication. It helps lay down a foundation for enhanced connections and general, all-round good feelings.

In biblical times and in all ancient religions, people offered gifts at the altar and partook of offerings of bread and wine as symbols of sacrifice. The gods gave their energies to the worshippers. The people gave of themselves to the deity concerned. As Jewish commentaries have pointed out, the Hebrew word for sacrifice, significantly, means "drawing nearer," not just to God but to other people.* So in offering a special wine from one's cellar or bin, this "sacrifice" assists the process

* www.winespirit.org

149

of drawing closer to those who receive it. The deeply personal nature of the choices made and of the exchange itself only serve to enhance the underlying spirit that wine almost magically transmits.

Often, the wine we ultimately choose to share with friends will be a blend, perhaps of a Cabernet and a Merlot. Thus, grapes that come from the same wine region yet from different varietals, under different conditions and in possibly quite different soils, will unite and become something much more distinguished or delightful than any single vintage. Yet each retains its own "fingerprint." This is a potent reminder that when we meet with friends over such a wine – however varied our lives and experiences; our talents, callings, or personalities may be – the social mix, with its strengths and depths and its uniqueness, composes a far greater reality. Each can bring out the "flavor" or distinct "bouquet" of the other in a harmonious whole.

Certainly over wine, the various masks we wear, the barriers we erect, the stiffness of our arthritic-like defenses all gradually soften or melt away. Tensions and stresses ease, or are forgotten, as we put aside

The Spirituality of Wine

for a while the various outer roles we play in the game of life, and open to others our inner selves, our vulnerabilities and feelings. In the true heart-to-heart communication that so often occurs, our spiritual lives are fortified and encouraged to grow. Self-transcendence, the aim of any true spiritual yearning, happens almost unawares. Thus, it is not accidental that wine is very seldom the choice of those who drink alone – whose sole desire is escape and who abuse "spirits" when what they really need and unconsciously seek is Spirit. Wine is by nature intended for sharing and partnership, a partnership with people and a pairing with food.

Few things in life can compare with the experience of sitting at a table enjoying fine food and taking the time to share a glass of wine as we call to mind the highlights of days gone by; enquire after absent or mutually remembered friendships from other places, other moments; talk of other wines we have shared with those present; and know the gladness of a fresh memory to savor and store away. Such moments make us rich beyond compare. They are a part of the creation of our own souls and help us vibrate with the sheer joy of being alive. And the best news is that those moments can carry on throughout the whole of one's life. As the poet Thomas Moore reminds us so beautifully,

What though youth gave us love and roses,
Age still leaves us friends and wine.

BALANCE

Wine is as old as the thirst of [humanity],
not the physical thirst…but the heaven-sent thirst
for what will still our fear – that our mind be at peace;
and stir our sense and sensibility – that we shall
not ignore nor abuse God's good gifts –
wine not the least of them.

ANDRÉ L. SIMON – *WINES OF THE WORLD*

We all yearn deeply for a sense of poise and balance as we journey through the ups and downs of normal day-to-day experience. Since the days of Aristotle, and even before, philosophers have pondered what it means to achieve "just right" in our social interactions with one another. For Aristotle, it was "the golden mean" or balance between two extremes – too much eagerness for danger was rashness; too little was cowardice. Too much discipline for children was harshness; too little was indulgence and neglect. The ideal is one of balance.

The simple rule always to be kept in mind with wine is "Not too much; not too fast." It's a sound approach to most of life's real pleasures. Wine experts like to speak of a truly well-balanced wine – not too

The Spirituality of Wine

acidic, not too fruity, not "too anything"! In other words, "just right."

That's why a balanced wine is a powerful metaphor of, as well as an

agent towards, a truly balanced life lived to its fullest potential.

Epilogue

CARING FOR THE VINEYARD OF OUR HEARTS

In water one sees one's own face;
But in wine one beholds the heart of another.
OLD FRENCH PROVERB

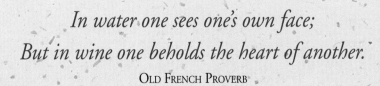

While in many ways organized religions are going through a difficult time just now, there has never been a time when the majority of people have been more aware that they are on a spiritual quest. Spirituality – or an emphasis on the inner life, on our crucial values and the question of what life truly is about – has become a leading concern as we move into this third millennium. The greatest spiritual teachers have always focused upon one central theme – and it applies to those who are religious as well as to those who are not.

What matters most is that we care for the vineyard of our heart. If we exercise the care in that crucial place that we give to other more material aspects of our lives, then like one who carefully tends a vineyard, we will eventually reap a harvest – a product of wisdom and love that blesses not just ourselves, but all those around us who "drink" of it.

Journalist and author George Saintsbury once wrote that when the vines he had tasted were good, "they pleased my senses, cheered my spirits, improved my moral and intellectual powers, besides enabling me to confer the same benefits on other people" (*Notes on a Cellar Book*, 1933).

Wine is water – plus a miracle. Vines can grow in some seemingly arid places; but they send their powerful roots deep into the earth and gravels beneath, seeking water from below, in the same way that they open their broad leaves to the rain and dew from above. Some of the best wines of antiquity came from the sun-baked gardens of old Egypt. Yet the River Nile was never far away. Vines and vineyards love to be close to water as, we have seen; remember the coast of "Vinland"; the rivers of France, Italy, and Germany; the shores of Lake Okanagan, Pelee Island, Lake Ontario, and the numerous other wine regions all around the world.

Water and a miracle. But so are we! Our bodies are roughly two-thirds water. For the ancient sages, water was ever and always a symbol

for matter itself. Humans, they taught, are a miraculous combination of matter and Spirit – and thus unique in all the animal creation. No wonder, then, that wine is such a powerful, sacramental, and universal symbol of the natural world – illumined and uplifted by the divine. Wine is water, plus spirit, it is true to say. It thus stands out among all the other products of the earth as a unique "nectar" blessed by the Spirit of the cosmos.

A Closing Toast

Here's to everyone:
To fullness of life on earth
and bounteous blessings for all humanity;
To justice, compassion, and
the warmth of the sun for all God's creatures;
To the golden health of loved ones everywhere,
and the radiant glory of those who have gone before.
God bless us now and evermore.
So be it.

Tom Harpur
Autumn Harvest, 2004

Whether expressed religiously or culturally, each time we raise a glass of wine…to wish each other well, we are introducing a moment and an experience that promotes wellness, balance and good health. It can only enhance our physical disposition even as it enriches our sense of connection and wholeness to all of the people and conditions that contribute to who we are and the journeys that we share.

WWW.WINESPIRIT.ORG

Bibliography

Aspler, Tony. *Vintage Canada*. 3rd edition. Toronto: McGraw Hill Ryerson, 1999.

Firefly Books. *A Wine Lover's Diary*. Toronto, 1999.

Frothingham, Andrew. *Great Toasts*. Franklin Lake, New Jersey: Career Press, 2002.

Fuller, Robert C. *Religion and Wine*. Knoxville, Tennessee: University of Tennessee, 1996.

Johnson, Hugh and Robinson, J. *The World Atlas of Wine*. London: Octopus Publishing Group, 2002.

Joseph, R. *K-I-S-S Guide to Wine*. New York: Dorling Kindersley Publishing Inc., 2000.

Kramer, Matt. *Making Sense of Wine*. Philadelphia: Running Press, 2003.

McCluskey, John William. *The Complete Book of Wedding Toasts*. Philadelphia: Arden Press, 2000.

Parker, Robert Jr. *Parker's Wine Buyer's Guide*. New York: Simon & Schuster, 2003.

Phillips, Rod. *A Short History of Wine*. London: Penguin Books, 2000.

Simon, André L. *Wines of the World*. New York: McGraw-Hill, 1962.

Taylor, Jennifer. *The Wine Quotation Book*. London: Robert Hale Limited, 1989.

Younger, William. *Gods, Men and Wine*. Cleveland, Ohio: World Publishing Co., 1966.

www.intowine.com/health.html

www.intowine.com/wine-toasts.html

www.winespirit.org (The Institute for the Study of Wine and Spirituality)

The Spirituality of Wine

Photographic Credits

Photos, used by permission, are listed below by page number.